D1831971

A
STUDY OF THE MAHAVASTU

A STUDY OF THE MAHAVASTU

BY

BIMALA CHURN LAW, Ph.D., M.A., B.L.,

WITH A NOTE BY DR. A BERRIEDALE KEITH, M.A., D.Litt., D.C.I., BAR-AT-LAW, REGIUS PROFESSOR OF SANSKRIT AND COMPARATIVE PHILOLOGY AT THE UNIVERSITY OF EDINBURGH

GYAN

Published by

GYAN

Gyan Publishing House
5, Ansari Road
Daryaganj, New Delhi-110002
Phone: 011-47034999, 9811692060
E-mail: books@gyanbooks.com

Distribution Network
gyanbooks.com
India, USA, Canada, UK, Australia, France

© Publisher

All rights reserved. No part of this work may be reproduced, stored, adapted, or transmitted in any form or by any means, electronic, mechanical, photocopying, micro-filming, recording or otherwise, or translated in any language, without the prior written permission of the copyright owner and the publisher.

ISBN : 978-81-212-2772-8 (HB)
First Published, 1930

2nd Impression 2021

Printed at: Gyan Press, Delhi.

The book is sold subject to the condition that it shall not, by way of trade or otherwise, be lent, resold, hired out, or otherwise circulated without the prior publisher's written consent.

A
Study of the Mahavastu
Author: Bimala Churn Law

A STUDY OF THE MAHĀVASTU

BY

BIMALA CHURN LAW, Ph.D., M.A., B.L.,

Calcutta University Gold Medalist, Sir Ashutosh Mookerjee Gold Medalist, Calcutta University. Corporate Member, American Oriental Society, Member, Royal Asiatic Society of Great Britain and Ireland, Advocate, High Court of Calcutta, Author, Some Kṣatriya Tribes of Ancient India, Ancient Mid-Indian Kṣatriya Tribes, Vol. I, Ancient Indian Tribes, Historical Gleanings, The Life and Work of Buddhaghosa, Women in Buddhist Literature, Heaven and Hell in Buddhist Perspective, Designation of Human Types, The Buddhist Conception of Spirits, etc. etc.

WITH A NOTE BY DR. A. BERRIEDALE KEITH, M.A., D.LITT., D.C.L., BAR-AT-LAW, REGIUS PROFESSOR OF SANSKRIT AND COMPARATIVE PHILOLOGY AT THE UNIVERSITY OF EDINBURGH

CALCUTTA AND SIMLA:

THACKER, SPINK & CO.

1930

लाहावंशावतंसाय स्वर्गताय महात्मने ।
अम्बिकाचरणाख्याय सदा विद्यानुरागिणे ॥
जनकाय मयोत्सृष्टा सश्रद्धं मत्कृतिर्मुदा ।
महावस्त्ववदानस्य समालोचनरूपिका ॥

CONTENTS

INTRODUCTION

The Mahāvastu or an encyclopædia of Buddhist legends and doctrines is one of the important books of Mahāyana Buddhist literature. Thanks to the untiring zeal and indefatigable labour of the French savant, Mon. E. Senart, who first undertook to edit the book in three big volumes with useful introductions to them written in French. The book is now out of print and is very difficult to be had. Mahāvastu literally means a great thing. The prose portions of the text are written in mixed Sanskrit while the poems are written more in Prākrit than in mixed Sanskrit. No doubt the language is " an arbitrary and unstable mixture of Sanskrit, Pāli, and Prākrits ". In many places it is difficult to arrive at the correct interpretation. The arrangement of the topics discussed in the book is most disorderly and the text is full of repetitions. It contains an account of Buddha's life and teachings together with the stories of his previous births. Besides, several knotty points of Buddhism and Buddhist philosophy are treated in it. It claims to be a book of the Vinaya Piṭaka according to the Lokottaravādins, a branch of the Mahāsaṅghikas. It contains very little of the rules of the Vinaya. It undoubtedly requires care and patience to go through the entire text and give a substance of it—a task which I have attempted in this book.

Dr. A. Berriedale Keith has laid me under a debt of obligation by specially writing a valuable note containing many points of importance connected with a study of the Mahāvastu.

For illustrations and for kind permission to reproduce them, I am grateful to the Director-General of Archæology, India.

BIMALA CHURN LAW

43, *Kailas Bose Street*,
Calcutta, 17*th March*, 1930

A NOTE ON THE MAHĀVASTU

By Dr. A. B. Keith, D.C.L., D.Litt.

An indispensable preliminary to our comprehension of Buddhism is the careful analysis in detail of the great texts which mark for us at least important stages in the development of Buddhist thought. The *Mahāvastu*, though it is not unworthy of translation, is nevertheless one of those works which can for practical purposes be adequately and effectively represented by something more brief, in which what is valuable is less obscured by masses of unimportant detail, and we are fortunate in that Dr. Bimala Churn Law has undertaken the heavy burden of making available to us in English the substance of the *Mahāvastu*. *Mega biblion, Mega kakon*, was the verdict of Greece, and, if the greatness of the Buddha demanded so vast a treatise, we epigonoi, to whom Buddhism is not the end of striving and the sole object of interest, may be excused if we prefer something more condensed and vital.

Of the interest and importance of the *Mahāvastu* there is no doubt; it has the fascination that almost everything that is definite has yet to be discovered regarding it. Its essential character remains a matter of dispute. It claims to be a book of the Vinayapiṭaka according to the text of the Lokottaravādins, a branch of the Mahāsaṅghikas, and this claim fortunately does not contradict any evidence otherwise available. But, as we have it, the work gives hardly any of the rules of the Buddhist community, which we expect from its claim to be its content. It corresponds instead to that part of the Pāli Vinayapiṭaka which tells of the history of the coming into being of the community, and we must hold either that the Vinaya itself was still preserved by the school in some older form of speech, or that it originally followed on the *Mahāvastu*, as we have it, but for some reason or other has perished. Either suggestion is open to serious difficulties but it is clear that it would be absurd to suppose that the Lokottaravādins were content to regard our *Mahāvastu* as representing the Vinaya of their school, even if we admit that the extent of the *Mahāvastu* suggests that they were lacking in a sense of proportion.

The tradition which regards our Pāli texts as representing the true doctrine of the Buddha treats the Mahāsaṅghikas as the first schismatics; but this powerful school, whose strength is indicated by its name, would doubtless have repudiated any suggestion that it did not preserve the true doctrine, and the same view would have been maintained by the school of the Lokottaravādins, or Transcendentalists, of the Middle Country, the land between the Himālaya and the Vindhya. To them the Buddha was no mortal teacher, differing in nothing save superior insight from ordinary man; seers like the Buddhas stand above the world, though they accommodate their actions to its life; if they wash their feet, yet dust stains them not, if they sit in the shade, yet the rays of the sun oppress them not, if they eat, yet hunger assails them not. It is in entire harmony with this view of the nature of the Buddha that full acceptance is accorded to the doctrine of the existence of Buddhas on a wholesale scale, and that we are assured that the purity of the Buddha is such that reverence paid to him suffices to win Nirvāṇa, while abundant merit can be attained by the mere circumambulation of a Stūpa and the paying of homage by offerings of flowers. A Buddhānusmṛti (i. 163 ff) pays adoration to the Buddha in the same fashion as do the Brahmanical Stotras of Viṣṇu or Śiva, reminding us of the strong underlying theistic tendency of Indian thought. A feature little dwelt on in the Pāli Canon appears in the elaborate account (i. 63 ff) of the ten stages through which a Bodhisattva must pass in his advance to Buddhahood, a theme developed in the Mahāyāna texts, and, as in those texts, we are told that Bodhisattvas are not of mortal birth, but come spontaneously into existence as the result of their own merits.

But taken all in all, it is not so much for novel philosophic views that the *Mahāvastu* is attractive as for the rich variety of its literary content. There is in it no trace of arrangement by a master hand; confusion, practically inextricable, reigns, and the main theme, the legend of the Buddha, is constantly broken by the interpolation of a

Jātaka or Avadāna, or even a dogmatic Sūtra. Repetitions abound; the tale of the Buddha's birth is repeated no less than four times, and the same episode or Jātaka may appear first in prose, then in verse. Thanks to this wealth of material we can find abundant parallels to important passages already known to us in the Pāli Canon. Thus we have an old version of the famous legend of Siddhārtha's departure from his home, parallel with the account in the *Majjhimanikāya* (26 and 36); there are versions of the Pabbajjā, Padhāna and Khaggavisāṇa Suttas of the *Suttanipāta*, of the *Khuddakapāṭha*, of the Sahassavagga of the *Dhammapada*, of the great sermon at Benares, of the Mahāgovinda Sutta of the *Dīghanikāya*, of the Dīghanakha Sutta of the *Majjhimanikāya*, etc. We have old ballads regarding the birth of the Buddha, which carry us back to the early days of the faith; we have also parallels for the late *Vimānavatthu* and *Buddhavaṁsa*. The Jātakas and similar tales, which make up a good half of the text, present us with the familiar picture of the Bodhisattva as now a king exercising universal sovereignty, now a merchant's son, a Brāhman, a Nāga prince, or the king of beasts; the stories constantly present close analogy with those in the Pāli Jātaka book, differing often in significant detail, or presenting important variation of substance; thus the Kusa Jātaka is told once (iii. 1ff) in a metrical version showing close connection with the Gāthās of the Pāli Jātaka (531) and once (ii. 420 ff) with marked variation.

The value of these semi-parallels is very great; thus the tale of Nalinī and Ekaśṛṅga as it appears in the *Mahāvastu* (ii. 143 ff) is no more than a pious and edifying legend of no special interest, yet it preserves some traces of antiquity which have disappeared from the Pāli legend of Isisiṅga, in the Nalinikā Jātaka. Other tales remind us of Brahmanical literary tradition and breathe the spirit of the Purāṇas. The childless Brahmadatta (i. 272 ff) has recourse to the seers, and three birds are born for him, who speak with human voices and deliver sayings of wisdom; the seer Rakṣita attains as a hermit such magic powers that he can touch the sun and the moon with his hands (i. 283 ff); the royal genealogy of Śākyamuni begins with the normal account of the creation (i. 338 ff). There are parallelisms between the account of the hells at the beginning of the *Mahāvastu* and that of the Mārkaṇḍeya Purāṇa, which testify to the inter-relation of the Buddhist and Brahmanical schools of thought. From the point of view of literary form we have a certain parallelism between the Jātakas of the *Mahāvastu* and the Pāli Canon; some of the *Mahāvastu* legends are in prose, some in prose with verses intermingled, some in prose, followed by verses covering practically the same ground.

Such a work, it is plain, cannot be the product of one period, and it is as necessary as it is difficult to seek to resolve it into its constituent parts. The language offers some aid in the process; the whole is written in what may for lack of a better term be styled "mixed Sanskrit", but this form of language is not the same throughout; in part it approximates more closely to Sanskrit proper, and it is doubtless plausible to hold that, as a rule, the more correct the diction the later the text in its present form, as opposed to the matter. This view is based on the belief that "mixed Sanskrit" represents an effort on the part of those, who used in their intercourse and teaching a Prākrit of some sort, to adopt Sanskrit as the language of their sacred texts, their success, however, being at first strictly limited. The alternative view is that which regards "mixed Sanskrit" as representing a genuine development in some form of proto-Sanskrit, and it is a striking proof of our imperfect knowledge of the early development of language in India that we are unable definitely to disprove this view. But, even if we adopt it, it would seem probable that the passages written in a language more closely approximating to Sanskrit are later than those which show more freedom, and the test of language, therefore, is probably valid. Unfortunately however, it carries us but a little way. Nor can we derive much aid from references of a historical character, for these are few and far between. The halo of the Buddha carries the passage in which it is mentioned down to the Christian era, for it indicates influence by the sculpture of Gandhāra. It is much more doubtful whether we can hold that we are carried down to the fourth century A.D. for those passages in which the Huns occur, Chinese speech and writing are alluded to, and the Yogācāras are mentioned; the Huns are known to the *Mahābhārata* and we are probably mistaken if we assume that their name penetrated to India only in the fourth or fifth century A.D.; the date of the term Cīna is still uncertain and problematic, and the Yogācāras (i. 120) are in all likelihood not the idealist school which later bears that style. We are on firmer footing when we find the term Horāpāṭhaka applied to an astrologer (iii. 178), for we are reasonably assured that the term Horā in this use was not known to India before the third century A.D.

A far more fruitful source of discrimination between the elements of the work is presented by stylistic considerations, attention to which was first definitely drawn by Oldenberg (*Nachrichten von der Königl. Gesellschaft der Wissenschaften zu* Göttingen, 1912, pp. 123ff.), in continuation of E. Windisch's important treatise, *Die Komposition des Mahāvastu*. He distinguishes between two distinct styles (A and B): the former is marked formally by the predominance of the nominal style, in which the copula is often omitted, and participles in —*ta* take the place of finite verbs. Such verbal forms as occur are usually in the present, and are often common word such as *bhavanti* or *gacchanti*. Sentences are frequently combined by the particle *dāni*, often following some form of derivative of the pronominal base *ta*, as in *so dāni*, *tatra dāni*. The

B style, on the other hand, uses freely finite verbal forms, including many past tenses; the nominal style is rare in narrative, more frequent when a speaker or thinker lays down some statement of fact. Dāni as a particle of connection is rare, while, on the other hand, *atha khalu* frequently serves this end, and an answer to a question or speech is frequently prefaced by *evam ukte*. Frequent also is the taking up of a narrative tense by a gerund or participle corresponding. Nor is the distinction between the styles formal only; the A style is far superior to the B style; its movement is free and unfettered, the structure of the sentence changes freely, it expresses much in little space, and in its long compounds it can compress a vast amount of matter, though with the usual risk of ambiguity. The B style, on the other hand, is stiff and monotonous; it occupies much space in telling little; it abounds in repetitions, and it lacks the power of subordination; the essential is described with no more emphasis than the idle detail of the mode in which the actors are dressed, meet one another, and sit down beside one another. There can be no doubt as to the true parallels of the two styles; A reminds us of the *Tantrākhyāyika*, B of the Pāli Canon, and stylistic grounds alone suggest the earlier date of passages in the B style. Confirmation may be drawn from the nature of the subject-matter of the passages in which either style is used. The B style is often found in passages for which we have Pāli parallels, the A style in passages which suggest additions and workings up of simpler accounts, narratives, or descriptions; it is in an A passage that Horāpāṭhaka occurs. From this we may deduce the conclusion that the *Mahāvastu* represents the working over of material which is preserved to us often in a simpler and more primitive form in the Pāli Canon, though neither the *Mahāvastu* nor that Canon can be said to represent faithfully the oldest Buddhist Canon in Māgadhī or Old Ardhamāgadhī.

Oldenberg admits that there has been much admixture of style through working over, and he distinguishes among the B passages a number (B[1]) which have no Pāli parallels but represent later work on the B model, such as the first Avalokita Sūtra (ii. 257–293). In his view Sūtra and Vinaya materials of this kind, in part parallel with the Pāli texts, in part later developments in the old style, were worked up into a whole with additions by an author using style A. The suggestion is attractive and ingenious, but the facts are extremely complex, and we may seriously doubt whether the redaction of the main body of the work apart from smaller interpolations such as the second Avalokita Sūtra (ii. 293–397) which admits itself to be a supplement, was the work of one hand. But for a decision on these and on many other points the time is not ripe; least of all can we say how far the doctrines of the *Mahāvastu* as it stands represent the views of the Lokottaravādins pure and simple, how far they are

Mahāyāna ideas adopted by that school or simply interpolated in their great text. Sufficient has been said to show how important and how interesting the study of the *Mahāvastu* is from the point of view of philosophy and literature alike.

PART I

CHAPTER I

The Buddhas and the Bodhisattvas

The Mahāvastu begins with an enumeration of the attributes of the Bodhisattvas, especially with regard to their conduct (caryā). In the first section obeisance is made to the past Buddhas by whom the present Buddha, *viz.*, Śākyamuni of Kapilavastu, was initiated and perfected gradually in his Buddhahood. The Bodhisattvas are characterised by four kinds of conduct befitting them and these are Prakriticaryā, Pranidhānacaryā, Anulomacaryā, and Anivartanacaryā.[1] In a former birth when he was a Rājacakravarttī, a king of kings, Śākyamuni gained bliss by practising Prakriticaryā under Aparājitadhvaja Tathāgata. Next as a Śreṣṭhin or leading merchant practising Praṇidhānacaryā he prayed to Atīta or the past Śākyamuni for the root of good conduct. He thought that he too would be a Perfectly Enlightened One in future. The city of Kapilavastu

[1] These terms are explained in the body of the text a few pages below. According to Mon. Senart, caryā means careers or degrees of the Bodhisattvas. Prakriticarya is that where the native qualities are being showed; Praṇidhānacaryā, where they take the vow to reach the bodhi or enlightenment; Anulomacaryā, where the conduct conformable to that vow is practised; Anivartanacaryā, where the preparation is done without running the risk of any forfeiture. Kern defines caryā as course. According to him, Prakriticaryā is original course, Praṇidhānacaryā is the course of the vow or firm resolution, Anulomacaryā is the course in accordance with the vow taken and Anivartanacaryā is the course in which no sliding back is possible.

would be his birth place and everybody would know him as Śākyamuni. Then as a Rājacakravarttī again, Śākyamuni practising Anulomacaryā prays to Samitāvin Tathāgata. Last of all obeisance is shown to Dīpaṅkara Tathāgata who said to Śākyamuni, "O, disciple, you will, in future, be famous as Śākyamuni Tathāgata, and fully enlightened. Those who follow the tenfold righteous path come nearer to the knowledge of truth."

Dīpaṅkara

Once the Buddha went to Dīpaṅkara Buddha who was then surrounded by an assembly of disciples and thought, "it would be better if I could be born to do good to mankind". Dīpaṅkara Buddha coming to know of his intention said, "You will, in future, be born in the Śākya family and for the good of mankind you will attain Buddhahood".

With a view to secure the good of mankind, Śākyamuni began to practise Bodhisattvācaryā and laboured for his own soul and the people. He practised dāna (charity). He thought of happiness and misery as of equal value. He began to spend his days in good deeds. He stayed free from attachment and enjoyment. Gradually he attained heaven, and found it transient; he practised severe austerity for final emancipation from this chain of births and deaths and taking his bath in the Nerañjarā river[1] he stayed fearlessly in the town of Gayā.

---

[1] Phalgu River in Gayā.

Purifying his heavenly eyes during the first watch of the night he thought of the movement of animals; during the middle watch he thought of the knowledge of former existence; during the last watch he discussed matters which must be known by everybody and thus he attained Buddhahood.

While the Lord Sanunāsambuddha was at Śrāvastī, at the Jetavana of Anāthapiṇḍika, he instructed gods and men. Thera Mahāmaudgalyāyana who had been roaming about in the hells came to Jetavana and described the horrible scenes he had witnessed at the eight nirayas or hells. He saw beings without number suffering in hell. In the Sañjīva hell he noticed some with their feet turned upwards and with heads hanging downwards, some being hewn and split with axes, others being torn by sharp instruments of iron (āyasonakha) and cut up by swords. In the Kālasūtra hell too, he noticed beings subjected to similar punishments. In the Saṅghāta hell he noticed beings tortured or crushed by mountains piled up upon them. In the Raurava hell he found thousands of beings subjected to countless varieties of punishments. In the Mahāraurava hell he found some beings thrown into the blazing fire and crying at the top of their voice. Their shrieks seemed to reach the ears of the people of Yambudvīpa,[1] Pubba-Videha, Aparagodāniya and

[1] The continent of India.

Uttarakuru.[1] He found many beings suffering in the Tapana hell where thousands of flames of fire blazing forth in their fury from the east spread up to the walls of the west, and again flames rising in the west stretching their fiery tongues up to the east. These and thousand other varieties of punishments and sufferings were inflicted upon beings in the innumerable hells, and there Mahāmaudgalyāyana described in the presence of the people assembled.

The description of hell was finished and everybody was struck with awe and amazement. But the great sage proceeded to give further details of these hells. He went on, "Acts productive of the knowledge of Truth ought to be performed. Sinful deeds of every kind should be avoided. The eight hells are *Sañjīva*, *Kālasūtra*, *Saṅghāta*, *Raurava*, *Mahāraurava*, *Mahāavīci*, *Tapana*, and *Pratāpana*[2]. Horrible scenes of every conceivable and inconceivable kind are seen in those terrible abodes of punishment. Persons who stir up enmity with others with regard to land, or any other thing, go to the Sañjīva hell. The arms of persons who entertain a desire to kill domestic animals are pierced with nails made of iron. Persons who order the cutting off of the trunks and legs of fetterred elephants go to the Kālasūtra

[1] See my paper on Uttarakuru, published in the Saṁkalpa.

[2] For a detailed account of hells and the description of them in the Mārkaṇḍeya Purāṇa, see my book, "Heaven and Hell in Buddhist Perspective".

(hell) where they are cut off from head to foot like sugarcane sticks. The Saṅghāta hell is of wide extent. There is a mountain cave area in the hell; when the warders of this hell armed with the instruments of torture seek the sinful inhabitants of this region, they hide themselves inside the cave, but at that time fire appears before them; and forced to come back through fear, they are followed by torrents of blazing fire. They are then pounded or crushed by mountains. Those who take away the life of animals including even the small insects have to go to this hell. Thus in other hells as well people have to undergo great sufferings".

Next Mahāmaudgalyāyana roamed about observing the painful conditions in which the lower animals had to pass their life and then reviewing their life of suffering gave an account of the miseries that they were subject to. Hay and wet grass were their food; water cold and hot their drink, they were harmful to one another; at every step they were in danger. At Jetavana he narrated in detail all these sufferings of the lower animals and impressed upon the audience that knowledge of truth should be acquired and sinful acts should be avoided, so that man may not run the chance of being reborn as any of the lower animals. Next he went about observing the condition of the pretas or spirits of the dead and found that the pretas suffer from intolerable miseries. Their mouths are like needles, the throats are choked, they know no satisfaction. The wind blows, water flows, food is before them but they have no power of enjoying these things owing to the consequence of their deeds when in life. They go forward with an intent to enjoy these articles of pleasure but they have to come back sorely disappointed.

Maudgalyāyana narrated the sufferings of the pretas before the audience at Jetavana and said that every one should acquire knowledge of truth and avoid sinful acts, so that they may not have to be reborn in that state.

Then the great sage Maudgalyāyana observed the condition of the Asuras (demons). At the abode of the Asuras he found them to be of huge body, horrible in appearance and always eaten up with envy at the greater comforts and pleasures of the devas or gods.

The Asuras think that they have been placed below and the gods above. Burning with fury at this thought, they besiege the abode of the gods with an entire army made up of four divisions, viz., elephants, chariots, horse and foot; and fight with the gods and go to hell after being killed in the combat. Coming to Jetavana Maudgalyāyana narrated the miseries of the Asuras that had their abode in the great ocean and many people took to the path of salvation.

Reviewing the condition of the Cāturmahārājika[1] devas or gods inhabiting the lowest of the

---

[1] The gods who are subjects of four guardian angels of four quarters.

six *devalokas*, Maudgalyāyana observes that while in this heavenly abode the beings enjoy various sorts of happiness, at the end of their period of pleasure and comfort, they fall down from heaven, and have to be reborn as *Pretas or Asuras* or as lower animals or to go to one or other of the hells. So these devas are also not immune from misery. Therefore, people should try to acquire knowledge of truth and should not commit sin. Arriving at Jetavana, Maudgalyāyana narrates his experiences and the people took to the path of salvation. Then again, reviewing the condition of the *Trayastiṁsa devas*,[1] Maudgalyāyana found that they were longlived, strong and happy. They roamed in the heavenly regions and drank nectar living in jewel-bedecked and beautiful palaces and playing in eight gardens, viz., *Vaijayanta*, *Nandāpuṣkarinī pārīpātra*, *Kovidāra*, *Mahāvana*, *Pāruṣyaka*, *Citraratha*, *Nandana and Misrakāvan.*

Śākra, the lord of gods, played in the Vaijayanta palace surrounded by eighty thousand nymphs (Apsarās). Thera Mahāmaudgalyāyana saw the splendid and prosperous city of the gods (Sudarsanaṁ devanagaraṁ) and the heavenly council (*Sudharmāṁ devasabhāṁ* or the Motehall of the gods), extending over thousand yojanas and gave an account of the sort of heavenly bliss that he had found them enjoying on his return

---

[1] Gods dwelling in the Tāvatiṁsa Heaven, *vide* my book, "Heaven and Hell in Buddhist Perspective" pp. 7 foll.

to Jetavana. At their will the devas enjoyed the blessings of heaven, but on the expiry of the term during which their merits acquired in past births entitled them to partake of these pleasures, they were born in the womb of lower animals and suffered. So the state of the gods was not quite enviable; it was mutable and transitory. So everybody should acquire knowledge of truth, perfect knowledge of Truth, supreme Buddhahood, do noble deeds, practise celibacy, and should not commit sin.

Maudgalyāyana next went to the other heavenly abodes, viz., those of the *Yāma*, *Tuṣita*, *Nirmāṇarati*, *Paranirmitavaśavarttī*, and *Brahmakāyika gods up to the region of the Suddhāvāsa devas.*[1] He found that they were long lived, virtuous, full of happiness, they moved in the sky, spoke sweet words, and that they were free from affections or passions, etc.

The Thera came back to Jetavana and narrated everything that he had seen in the abodes of the gods and observed that even their happy state though apparently so free from pain was not permanent; ultimately it was liable to a change. He impressed the truth that all people have faults, all the worlds are full of misery and impermanent, so the Buddhas teach Dharma, so as to reach a permanent and stable state of existence and to acquire the highest good.

[1] For a detailed account see my book "Heaven and Hell in Buddhist Perspective."

Then he asked the assembly to acquire knowledge of truth, perfect knowledge of truth, to do noble deeds, to practise celibacy, and to refrain from committing sinful deeds. Many people listened to these words of the Thera and tasted the bliss of eternal life.

Gautama

The Lord, the Perfectly Enlightened One, thought of his mission, came to the Gṛdhrakūṭa hills at Rājagṛha, and was honoured by both gods and men. He taught them to be disinterested. He distributed knowledge amongst the people of *Aṅga*, *Magadha*, *Vajjī*, *Malla*, *Kāśī*, *Kośala*, *Cedi*, *Vatsa*, *Matsya*, *Sūrasena*, *Kuru*, *Pañcāla*, *Sivi*, *Daśārṇa*, *Aśvaka*, and *Avanti* [1] and had magnificent *vihāras* erected for him. Once Mahāmaudgalyāyana went to Rājagṛha for alms. He thought it was a long time since he had been to the holy abode of the gods. Thinking thus he went on foot to the holy abode of the gods. The sons of the gods of paradise saw longlived Mahāmaudgalyāyana from a distance and proceeded forth to receive him and said, "O, long-lived one, welcome!" Thus they received him with greetings, saluted him, and took their seat. One of the sons of the gods said to Mahāmaudgalyāyana, "Long ago there lived in the city of Vasumata a bhikṣu named Abhiya during whose life-time, the city was the prosperous abode of many happy people. A rich Brahmin named

[1] Vide my books, "Some Kṣatriya Tribes of Ancient India", "Ancient Mid-Indian Kṣatriya Tribes, Vol. 1," and "Ancient Indian Tribes".

Uttiya also lived in this city. He associated with such Bhikṣus as Nanda and Abhiya. When, however, Nanda and Abhiya would pay a friendly visit to the house of Uttiya, Nanda was honoured more than Abhiya. One of the daughters of Uttiya was the wife of a certain merchant of Vasumata. She too was pleased with Nanda. Abhiyabhikṣu was jealous of Nanda and traduced the character of Nanda with false report that Nanda had lost *Brahmacaryā*.[1] As a result of this report, the Brahmin householders and the merchant did no longer honour him as they used to do previously. After a few days Abhiya repented of his sinful act of spreading calumny against Nanda of pure character. He then begged pardon of Nanda and made his wrong deed known to the world." Abhiya went to the merchant Uttiya and said, "I want mastery over the assembly of Buddhist disciples, enjoyed by the Lord. Give me money". Uttiya and other householders gave him gold. Two gandhikas (dealers in perfumes) of Vasumata were very pleased with Abhiyabhikṣhu. Abhiya did what he liked with that money. Then Abhiyabhikṣu thought that he would try to become Perfectly Enlightened, to be free and make people free, to be consoled and console others, to restrain himself and make others restrained. The Supreme Lord or the All Highest came to know of his good intention and said to him, "You will acquire perfect knowledge

[1] Leading a holy life.

and become Śākyamuni Tathāgata. Gods and men will take advice from you".

"Endowed with the thirty-two signs of a great man[1] and the ten powers of a Tathāgata[2] and the four Vaiśāradyas[3] or subjects of confidence or fearlessness, you will gain excellence. In future you will set the wheel of Dharma[4] rolling, which has not yet been done by any Śramaṇa or god or Māra.[5] You will do good to gods and men in innumerable ways."

"Give that gift and resolve, I shall be the priest of gods and men and preach the noblest religion. Beat the flagged drum of Dharma, elevate the divine sage, sound the sacred conches,

---

[1] The thirty-two signs of a great man or 32 Mahāpuruṣa lakṣaṇas. See 'A Manual of Buddhism by R. Spence Hardy', pp. 368-369.

[2] The balas or potentialities are: (1) Knowledge of what is fit or unfit, (2) of the necessary consequences of Karma, (3) of the right road leading to any end, (4) of the elements, (5) of the different inclinations of beings, (6) of the relative powers of the organs, (7 and 8) of all degrees of meditation and ecstasy as well as of their power to purify and gratify the mind, (9) of remembering former births, (10) of removing moral corruption (Kern's Manual of Indian Buddhism, p. 62).

[3] Four Vaiśāradyas are: (1) assurance of the Buddha that he has got omniscience, (2) that he has freed himself from sin, (3) that he knows the obstacles in the way of attaining Nirvāṇa, (4) that he has shown the right path leading to Mukti or salvation.

[4] *Dharmacakra* is a symbol rather than a relic. It is undoubtedly an object of worship as Kern points out. One of the sculptures of the Bharhut represents the Buddha's Dhammacakka adorned with a strip of cloth under an umbrella in a shrine. Kern rightly points out that the wheel symbol is Buddhistic in so far as it is linked with the preaching of the doctrine. (Kern's Indian Buddhism, pp. 99.)

[5] See my paper on the Buddhist Conception of Māra (Proceedings and Transactions of the Third Oriental Conference, Madras, 1925, pp. 483 foll.) and Buddhistic studies edited by Dr. B. C. Law.

convert many people to the sacred religion. Let gods and men listen to my sweet words. Impart knowledge amongst the people oppressed by births and deaths; release people who are on the way to hell, do good to people by imparting counsel like the Buddha; being free I shall turn the wheel of Dharma."

The omnipresent and Perfectly Enlightened One came to know of his intention and said that in future he would be a *jina*[1] (Conqueror).

Then in future when the gandhikas heard of Perfect Enlightenment of Abhiyabhikṣhu, they decided to accept the discipleship of the Buddha on his attaining perfect enlightenment.

Abhiyabhikṣhu exerted for a long time for perfect truth. He worshipped Arahats (saints) who had acquired perfect knowledge. They said nothing to him. He worshipped three hundred arahats by the name of Puṣpa. They did not say anything. He worshipped innumerable Buddhas. They said nothing to him. He spoke of the four kinds of the conduct of the Bodhisattva, viz., Prakriticaryā, Praṇidhānacaryā, Anulomacaryā, and Anivarttanacaryā. To worship the present Buddha and to pay respects to the disciples of the Buddha and to follow the right path is the principle involved in Prakriticaryā or the observance of the natural state. Praṇidhānacaryā is

---

[1] Jina means a Buddha, a Sugata, or a Tathāgata. It literally means a Conqueror.

the right realisation of the doctrine of Śākyamuni.

When such persons will acquire virtue by purifying their body and mind, their minds will gain Bodhi or the Supreme knowledge. They will think thus, "We shall gain omniscience by virtue of meritorious deeds and our meditation may not be disturbed. Let the roots of meritorious acts which we have accumulated be beneficial to all people. Let evil come upon us for our sinful acts. Being possessed of a mind unaffected by worldly thoughts we shall roam over the whole world, we shall turn the unique wheel of religion which is honoured by gods and men alike".

Samitāvi

Then in the course of innumerable kalpas, Samitāvi became a Perfectly Enlightened Tathāgata. He became an instructor of gods and men. At this time Vijitāvī, lord of the four island-continents, possessed of the seven gems, virtuous and engaged in the path of ten-fold meritorious action, ruled as king over the earth. The seven treasures are cakraratna (the magic wheel of a Cakravarttī monarch, which rolls before him when he makes his royal tour from one continent to another), Hastiratna (the elephant), aśvaratna (the horse), maniratna (the gem), strīratna (the empress), gṛhapati ratna (the retinue of householders), parināyakaratna (the crown prince). A thousand sons were born to him. They were brave, powerful, and handsome and victorious over alien armies. That the king began to rule over the world, up to Jambudvīpa, East Videha, Aparagodāniya, and the Uttarakuru, without having to exercise the rod, the kingly weapons, and without oppression. Then once the king came to Cakravarttī Samitāvi and cleaned robes, almsbowl, bed and seat and built a palace bedecked with the seven gems. Close to the palace he built eighty-four thousand pillars, set with gold, silver, pearl, and all sorts and varieties of the most precious gems in the world. He built eighty-four thousand kuṭāgāras (pinnacled houses) which were as beautiful as the palace bedecked with gems like those just mentioned. He thought, "I would become a perfectly enlightened one like Samitāvi. Being erudite I shall descend on earth as governor of gods and men. Bearing the thirty-two signs of a great man, versed in innumerable Buddhist doctrines, endowed with the ten-fold power of the Tathāgata, having the four Vaiśāradyas or subjects of confidence, I shall console others and shall console myself, I shall help people to attain Nirvāṇa and myself shall attain Nirvāṇa. I shall do such deeds as will be beneficial to mankind."

"I shall move in this world with minds unaffected by worldly affairs like this Samitāvi and shall turn the wheel of law being worshipped by gods and men."

Then the perfectly enlightened Samitāvi thought thus, "After how long a time will Buddha be born? The Buddha is not seen in one Kalpa or in two

Kalpas. He is seen once in a thousand Kalpas". Then he became kind to all people. Five-fold Buddhacaryā became his essential duties. The five-fold Buddhacaryās are (1) to turn the wheel of law as a duty, (2) mild behaviour towards mother, (3) mild behaviour towards father, (4) conversion of people into the Buddhist faith, (5) and celebration of the sprinkling ceremony of a prince.

Ajita

Buddha named Ajita was of Maitra gotra in Bandhuma capital. He invited the bhikṣus and said, "A thought, when the Buddha will be born, has crossed my mind. I want to live for thousands and thousands of years: is there any bhikṣu who likes to live with me?"

All of them cried out or replied "Lord! we shall be with you".

When Vijitāvi was ruling as Cakravarttī[1] and lord of the four island-continents and as the conqueror of the four island-continents by virtue of merit, the Perfectly Enlightened Samitāvi was established in the long course of life with the Śrāvakas (disciples). When he came to know that the span of human life was limited and that human beings are on the way to old age, disease and death, then Samitāvi with his disciples came to Jambudvīpa and began to preach religious counsels. Then Vijitāvi got palaces built for the Perfectly Enlightened Samitāvi. Thus elapsed many a Kalpa in prayer for Perfect Enlightenment. Thus I have

---

1 Universal monarch.

heard: the Lord was once staying on the Gṛdhrakūṭa mountain at Rājagṛha. At that time Mahāmaudgalyāyana was wandering for alms with his robes and alms-bowl. Desirous of going to the sacred abode of the gods he went to the sky; the sons of gods saw him come up the firmament. They went towards the spot where Maudgalyāyana was coming, and bowing down they took their seats. They began to say thus in verse, "After a hundred thousand years having acquired matured knowledge (Bodhi or enlightenment) the Lord Buddha was born in the world". Saying this the gods of the holy abode saluted Maudgalyāyana and took their seats on one side. Then waiting for sometime on one side they disappeared. Then Mahāmaudgalyāyana thought of various things and then disappearing from that place he came to Rājagṛha. Then after wandering for alms in Rājagṛha, he kept his robes and alms-bowl and washing his feet he saluted the Lord, took his seat on one side and narrated every thing in detail. Then he said, "Lord! I put to you questions regarding Perfect Enlightenment". The Lord then said, "Innumerable Tathāgatas in innumerable kalpas (cycles) have eradicated the (root or) principle of sin. They pray for the highest enlightenment. I worshipped thirty koṭis of Buddhas named Śākyamuni with their disciples. When I was a Cakravarttī king, these Buddhas told me that I would become the ruler of gods and men, and would be a Perfectly Enlightened Tathāgata

Arahat. I know hundred thousands of Dīpaṅkara Mahābuddhas whom I honoured with their disciples. They told me that I would attain Buddhahood in future. I know five hundred Buddhas named Padmottara; I know eight thousand Buddhas named Paddyotas; I know three koṭis of Buddhas named Puṣpa; I know eighteen thousand Buddhas named Māradhvaja to whom I used to pray for the highest enlightenment, practising Brahmacaryā or restraint. They gave me much advice. I served five hundred Buddhas named Padmottara with their disciples. I know nine thousand Buddhas named Kāśyapa, fifteen thousand Buddhas named Kauṇḍinya and each and every one of the eighty-four thousand Buddhas.

I know the Perfectly Enlightened One named Samantagupta, thousand Buddhas named Yambuddhvaja, eighty-four thousand Buddhas named Indraddhvaja, sixty-two hundred Buddhas of different names, sixty-four Buddhas named Samitāvi. I know the Perfectly Enlightened Buddha named Suprabhāsa where Maitreya, Bodhisattva and Vairocana being Cakravarttī, first uprooted the three evil principles."

Suprabhāsa

When Suprabhāsa became Tathāgata, the span of human life became eighty-four koṭi thousand years. Suprabhāsa formed three Saṁghas or assemblies of Śrāvakas or disciples. The first Saṁgha was formed with ninety-six koṭis of arahats, and the second with ninety-four koṭis of arahats. King Vairocana was delighted to see Suprabhāsa. He served the Lord Suprabhāsa for ten thousand years and he too intended to be erudite and to attain the perfectly enlightened Buddhahood. He thought of becoming a religious teacher like Suprabhāsa. He would do good to mankind. Being a valiant Cakravarttī, he served with a desire for Perfect Enlightenment. On hearing those words Mahāmaudgalyāyana praised the words of the Lord.

Ratna

"In ancient times,"—continued the Buddha Gautama,—"there was a Perfectly Enlightened Buddha named Ratna. I was then a Rājcakravarttī. I got eighty-four thousand kūṭāgāras built for that Buddha. Those kūṭāgāras were set with seven kinds of precious minerals such as gold, silver, pearl, gems (as sapphire, ruby), cat's eye, diamond, and coral. Thus serving the Perfectly Enlightened Lord I was eager for knowledge. He told me everything about Perfect Enlightenment. This is Praṇidhicaryā or practice of profound meditation. 'O,' Mahāmaudgalyāyana, Anulomacaryā is to stay in an agreeable way for the understanding of the Bodhisattva. Anivartanacaryā is to understand the revolving in the circles of transmigration. For this ten bhūmikas[1] or stages are to be practised."

[1] The whole law of a Bodhisattva is divided into ten bhumis or stages. The Mahāvastu amply describes the system of bhumis. The most usual names are: (1) Pramuditā, Vimalā, Prabhākarī, Arciṣmatī, Sudurjayā, Abhimukhī, Duraṅgamā, Acalā, Sādhumatī or Madhumatī, and Dharmameghā. (See J.R.A.S., 1875, Daśabhūmīśvara.)

Kāśyapa

When the son of the Śākyas, bright like gold, passed away, the earth with her mountains shook. Then Kāśyapa noticed this, and revolving within himself as to why the earth had shaken found out that the Buddha had attained Nirvāṇa. He saw the Buddha attaining Nirvāṇa and the heavenly nymphs worshipping him and thought of following the Buddha on foot rather than with wealth. With this thought Kāśyapa went with a sorrowful heart with many bhikshus. Then four Mallas came with torch, but the torch was suddenly extinguished, at this everybody was astonished and asked the reason for the torch's sudden extinction. When Kāśyapa came there and bowed down to the Buddha at the time of the cremation of his body, all who were present began to give expression to their sorrow by saying that it was no good to live in this world for a long time and that they too should relinquish this body.

Then Kāśyapa began to advise them that they should act up to the behests of the Buddha, they should establish the wheel of religion in the Saptaparṇa cave at Rājgṛha in Magadha. Then all of them went up to the sky within a very short time and came to the forest by the side of a mountain and began to beat drums. At this all began to assemble.

"For the good of gods and men," said Kāśyapa, "I shall be free and shall free others, I shall establish the wheel of religion in Kāśipuri for the good of gods and men." The gods from the sky listened to the various words of Kāśyapa and said, "That's good, That's good. Thus continues the rule of the Buddha. One who is engaged for the good of mankind is an excellent man."

Kāśyapa instructed them regarding the five elements of being (Pañcaskandha). He regarded passion as a black serpent, and instructed people regarding passion as such. He realised eternal happiness. As a glow-worm loses its light with the sun-rise, so anti-Buddhists lose their brightness at the rise of the Buddha-sun. God acquires vision by virtue of the strength of the Jina (conqueror). Then Mahāmaudgalyāyana called long-lived Mahākāśyapa and said, "O, disciple of Buddha (Jinaputra), cause the doubtful mind of all to settle". Mahākāśyapa said to Aniruddha, Upāli, old Alakundalabhathiya, and Sundarananda, "O, disciples of Jina (Buddha)! Take care to study Psychology. Question every one as to any doubt that may be entertained by him". Then the disciples began to study the minds of other people. Kāśyapa said to Pranamvavāhu Vaśībhūta, "I shall build a palace to accommodate eighteen thousand people at the peak of the Gṛdhyakūṭa hill". He said to Vicintacūta Vaśībhūta, "I shall create clouds of Ganges water in the sky". He said to Haryakṣa Vaśībhūta, "Practise self-concentration". He said to Varuṇa Vaśībhūta, "Put an end to bitings and mosquitoes like dissatisfaction of mankind". He said to Ajakarṇa,

"Put an end to hunger, thirst, and disease". The disciples of the Buddha praised Kāśyapa on hearing him and went away.

Then Thera Kāśyapa said to Kātyāyana, "Narrate the biography of great men". Kātyāyana began to describe Buddhacaryā or the career of a Buddha, "There are ten bhūmikas or stages of the Bodhisattvas. The first one is named Durārohā, the second Vardhamānā, the third Puṣpamaṇḍitā, the fourth Rucirā, the fifth Cittavistarā, the sixth Rūpavatī, the seventh Durjayā, the eighth Yanmaniddesā, the ninth Yauvarājya, and the tenth Abhiṣeka". Kāśyapa again asked Kātyāyana to describe the results of the aforesaid stages. Kātyāyana said, "O, disciple! It is impossible to determine whether the stages of the Bodhisattvas are ten only or innumerable. The whole world is a stage by parts of the Bodhisattvas, so its name is stage (Bhūmi)". Then a Jinaputra named Ānanda said to Kātyāyana, "O, Jinaputra! If one of the stages be immeasurable or unknowable, then how can another stage be reached"? Kātyāyana replied, "It is the rule of the Supreme One that immeasurable advices are imparted in immeasurable kalpas. The wise Buddha by the influence of his intelligence has exhibited these stages. The remaining stages are known by slight hints".

Those who are on the first stage, are seen to have eight-fold practices, such as renunciation, kindness, complacency, humidity, proficiency in all the śāstras, prowess, command of men, and patience. Bodhisattvas attain the second stage only because of one reason which is experiencing enjoyment. They stay at the second stage for two reasons which are (1) absence of desire for sensual qualities, and (2) freedom from living on the interest on capital.

Again for three reasons, the Bodhisattvas stay on the second stage, as a Bodhisattva of the first stage attains the second stage in six different ways; *e.g.*, knowledge of impermanence.

Thus after many words Mahākāśyapa asked Mahākātyāyana, "How much merit arouses the desire to be a Perfectly Enlightened one?" Then Kātyāyana said, "Such a sacred desire is cherished by those disciples of Buddha who wishing to acquire perfect knowledge, give charity to those endowed with ten potentialities in Jambudvīpa, think lightly of wealth, and do good deeds to mankind". Mahākāśyapa asked Kātyāyana, "O disciple of Buddha! Do the Bodhisattvas acquire by virtue of their merit the earnestness of which you speak, or do they attain the above stage on the development of the roots of goodness (Kuśalamūlā)?" Kātyāyana said to Mahākāśyapa in verse, "First, man worships Tathāgata, [1] does not allow his mind to be attached to other things, then he thinks that

[1] It means 'one who has trodden the right path.' Vide my paper on "Data from the Sumaṅgalavilāsinī, Buddhaghosa's commentary on the Dīgha Nikāya of the Sutta Piṭaka." (J.A.S.B., New series, Vol. XXI, 1925, No. I. Article No. 10.)

he may acquire omniscience by virtue of the acquisition of the roots of goodness. Let good or evil deeds done by me be passed over".

Then Mahākāśyapa asked Kātyāyana, "What sort of strong prowess is acquired by the Bodhisattvas?" Mahākātyāyana said, "I shall not withdraw the state of mind by which I have acquired knowledge of perfection (paramārtha). I shall not hesitate to renounce birth, decrepitude, death, sorrow, and oppression. In this world work for money produces sorrow. This is the prowess of the Supreme man".

Mahākāśyapa asked Mahākātyāyana, "What wonderful virtue is gained by the Bodhisattvas at the first stage of concentration?" Mahākātyāyana said to Mahākāśyapa, "When supreme persons acquire the practice of profound meditation, a lustre like that of the sun shines. All sides are lit up. Gods begin to talk to each other thus: 'This person strives for being the foremost of men, is eager for the good of the world. So we should always save him'". Kāśyapa asked Kātyāyana, "What sort of difficult acts are done by the Bodhisattvas while on the above first stage?"

Kātyāyana began to reply to Kāśyapa, Doers of wonderful deeds, being established on the first stage, do not feel sorrow after giving away wife, happiness, children, head, eye, and ample dress. Because they are ready to be all-knowing. They use soft words to those who are inimical towards them. They do not repent after giving any good

3

thing. Their hope for worldly happiness disappears by virtue of the rules of penance.

The Bodhisattvas even when suffering bodily injury do not cherish anger; those who are foremost amongst human beings always think of doing good at heart. For the good of humanity, people should accumulate much merit. One should practise charity and be free from jealousy; one should show his fitness for gaining entrance into the paths with a mind well concentrated, one should not accumulate merit for the enjoyment of sensual pleasures. Those who are determined to be like the Buddhas should not be addicted to sensual pleasures. A person should hanker after the noble truth giving up all thoughts of earthly gain and honour. One should not covet the food of others even if he is put to dire strait. One should not cherish desires even if he is attached to the worldly life. Persons who are well-versed in all religions, and who have inclination to perform good deeds, are deemed to be good persons. In the Mahāvastu, all such persons are called by different epithets.

Persons who perform twenty-eight kinds of religious acts and who are in the second stage, go to the third stage, *e.g.*, (1) One who is satisfied with the acquisition of small merit, (2) One who is not jealous of others on account of his own form (beauty), etc., (3) One who holds garlands, garments, etc. Those who go from the second stage to the third one are bent upon self-sacrifice. They exert for the happiness of others and not for worldly happiness. They consider a good saying to be as precious as their son and wife.

A Brahmin went to a ṛṣi named Nareśvara and said, "There is a good saying (Subhāsita) which is equal in value to your helmet". The king took away his helmet and at his request the Brahmin communicated to him the good saying which runs thus, "If a person who has attained enlightenment and who is of good character, performs a demerit, it does not look well".

A rākṣasa went to a king named Surupa and said, "I have a good saying which I can sell to you in exchange for your prince, wife, and yourself". It is to be noted that the rākṣasa would devour them all. The meaning of that good saying is this, "It is better to stay in hell which is full of lamentations than to associate with a bad person". A demon told a minister named Sañjaya, "Give me your heart and I shall give you a good saying in exchange". Sañjaya consented. The meaning of that good saying is this, "As fire cannot be extinguished by grass or wood so desire cannot be removed by a person who is steeped in worldly affairs".

A poor man came to a banker named Vasundhara and spoke to him thus, "There is a good saying which can be exchanged for everything you possess". The banker consented and requested the poor man to relate the good saying which is as follows: 'The place where a fool dwells, appears to be empty even if it is inhabited by many men.

But the place where a wild person dwells appears to be fully inhabited even if it is actually vacant'.

A certain person went to a king named Surupa and offered to relate to him a good saying in exchange for the continent of India. Surupa promised to hand over the whole of the continent of India to him. At his request the following good saying was narrated: "The Tathāgatas appear in the place where pride, arrogance, etc., prevail in order to destroy them". A hunter told a deer named Sattara that if he could offer him his flesh, he could tell him a good saying. The deer consented and the hunter uttered the good saying which runs thus, "Dust of good men is very wholesome, but a golden mountain is not so, the dust removes sorrow, but the golden mountain increases it".

A servant of a king, named Nāgabhuja, told his master, "You can have a good saying in exchange of the Empire of four island-continents". The king consented and the servant uttered the good saying which is as follows: "A person feels slight pain if a hair of his body be uprooted. Such is the nature of the evil deed of a wise person. One should become the preceptor of the world by uprooting demerit by wisdom and by acquiring purity". Thus the foremost amongst the conquerors performs many difficult deeds for the sake of good sayings and thereby acquires fame.

Mahākâtyāyana questioned by Mahākāśyapa, told him that a person remaining in the third stage in fourteen forms goes to the fourth stage, *e.g.*, one who is unattached to dice-play, etc., one who finds delight in his own conscience, one who does not enjoy wealth though he is possessed of it, etc. Mahākātyāyana further said, "All creatures traversing the path of intelligence like sages, having acquired concentration of mind, enjoy all kinds of happiness".

A Bodhisattva named Nāmatideva saluted the Blessed One and uttered the following words: "One should salute a person who is endowed with thirty-two signs of a great man, who is noble in character, who has his senses under control, who is of serene mind, who is worshipped by gods and demons. One should salute the sage, who performs good deeds, who is compassionate and who has performed many good deeds in order to free himself from the worldly tie. One should salute the great sage who belonged to the Ikṣāku family and who enjoyed supreme happiness by renouncing worldly life. One should salute the chief of the Śākyas, who after giving up the Tuṣita heaven, entered into the womb of Queen Māyā and who was born later to save the creatures who are ignorant of true knowledge".

The character of Bodhisattvas

"The Bodhisattvas," said Thera Kātyāyana to Kāśyapa, "never disobey their parents and arahats. They never destroy stūpas, they never cherish ill feeling towards the Tathāgata, never perform evil deeds, are not attached to the world. They never cut the leaves of the tree which gives them shade. They do not sing such incantations as are destructive of human life. They never find much delight in wealth nor are they overwhelmed with sorrow at the time of danger. He who is the foremost amongst men performs deeds for the good of the world. Up to the eighth stage, the jinas, *i.e.*, conquerors, are unknown as Perfectly Enlightened Buddhas. As soon as they attain the eighth stage they take to deep meditation, they acquire supreme knowledge and they obtain pure birth. Gods, brahmins, and demons stand before them with folded hands on account of their virtues. The Bodhisattvas who are supreme rulers advise the people not to kill living beings and not to commit adultery. The Bodhisattva who is the lord of four islands obtains seven treasures. He acquires cakraratna, hastiratna, aśvaratna, turagaratna, maṇiratna, strīratna, gṛhapatiratna, and pariṇāyakaratna. Then he rules the kingdom righteously. The jinas who have acquired the fourth stage, pass on to the fifth stage and acquire seven kinds of state therein. They do not attach much importance to the bhikkhuṇīs. They bring about the ruin of good men and by means of the mantra they make others diseased. Those among the Bodhisattvas are the foremost, who are possessed of real intelligence. Kātyāyana questioned by Mahākāśyapa told the name, family name and span of life of the Perfectly Enlightened ones who acquired name and fame. In the Śākya family there was a Buddha named Yasobrata; he belonged to the family of Gautama; he lived for six thousand years; his aim was to obtain the noble truth, Paramārtha, by the merit accumulated by charity to the Arhat. There was a chief of men named Sudarśana; he belonged to the family of Bharadvāja. His influence extended over an area of ten yojanas. He had many koṭis of disciples. He acquired a long span of life by subduing Māra. There was a cakravarttī king named Dharanidhara who told Sudarśana that he would save the people who were subject to old age and death. There was a Buddha named Nareśvara. His influence extended over an area of ten yojanas and he belonged to the family of Vaśiṣṭha. At this time, the span of human life was nine thousand years. There was a Cakravarttī king named Aparājita. He offered many monasteries to the chief of men who was endowed with ten potentialities. He promised to acquire the strength of a jina by means of charity. An officer named Vijaya became a jina named Suprabha. He belonged to the family of Kāśyapa. His influence extended over an area of ten yojanas. He had eighteen koṭis of disciples. He invited the foremost of conquerors to a dinner at his house which he accepted. There was a Buddha named Ratṇaparvata. He belonged to the family of Gautama. His influence extended over an area of ten Yojanas. At his time, the span of life was for twenty thousand years.

At that time there was a king named Accyuta who offered thousand palaces to the Buddha and made up his mind to become a saviour of the poor by means of charity. There was a Buddha named Kanakaparvata. He belonged to the family of Kauṇḍinya. His influence extended over an area of six yojanas; the members of his family were five koṭis.

At this time there was a king named Priyadarśana. He was the lord of four islands; he gave in charity his kingdom named Kanakaparvata to the Buddha, and he resolved to acquire the state of the Buddha by means of charity.

Puṣpadanta of the Vatsa family

There was a Buddha named Puṣpadanta endowed with thirty-two signs of a great man. He belonged to the family of Vatsa or Vaṁśa. His influence extended over an area of nine Yojanas. He had thirty-four koṭis of disciples. At this time the span of life was fifty thousand years.

At this time there was a king named Durjaya. With his family he went to Puṣpadanta, worshipped him, and invited him to take his food for a week at his palace. Thus having pleased him the king made up his mind to become a Perfectly Enlightened Buddha like Puṣpadanta.

Lalitavikrama of the Vaśiṣṭha family

There was a Buddha named Lalitavikrama endowed with thirty-two signs of a great man. He belonged to the family of Vaśiṣṭha. His influence extended over an area of seven yojanas. He had thirty koṭis of disciples. At this time there was a king named Priyamanāpa who had a fourfold army. He built many small palaces made up of various gems and a big palace. Later on he made up his mind to become a Perfectly Enlightened Buddha in order to put an end to old age, death, etc.

Mahāyaśa of the Kāśyapa family

There was a Buddha named Mahāyaśa who was also endowed with thirty-two signs of a great man. He belonged to the family of Kāśyapa. His influence extended over an area of fifty yojanas. He had many disciples. At this time there was a king named Mṛgapatiśvara who pleased the Buddha very much and made up his mind to become all knowing like the Buddha.

Ratnacūḍa of the Bhāradvāja family

There was a Buddha named Ratnacūḍa. His influence extended over an area of one hundred yojanas. He belonged to the family of Bharadvāja. He had many disciples. At his time the span of life was eighty-four thousand years. At this time there was a king named Manivisāna. He built many palaces and offered them to the Buddha Ratnacūḍa. For ten years continually he fed Ratnacūḍa. Later on he made up his mind to save people who had given themselves up to worldly affairs. Thus we see that the jinas having acquired fame perform good deeds for the good of the world.

Mahākātyāyana further said to Mahākāśyapa,

"The jinas ascend to the sixth stage from the fifth stage in four forms, *viz.*, (1) living in association with Yogācāra, having been a follower of the Exalted Buddha, (2) giving up sensation, etc., (3) acquiring tranquillity, insight, contemplation, etc., and (4) contemplating with a concentrated mind".

Kātyāyana added, "The duty of a Buddha is to fulfil the Karma of the Buddha which is difficult to perform. If a Buddha is incapable of finishing all work, two Buddhas arise".

Kātyāyana names a good many jinas (conquerors), *e.g.*, Mṛgapatiskandha, Sinhahanu who was endowed with thirty-two signs of a great man, Lokaguru and he further names the Buddhas, Jñānadhvaja, and Devanandita. There was a king named Kuśa in the seventh stage and he had a queen named Apratimā. There was also a king named Jaṭhara who heard of Apratimā and being desirous of winning her, sent a messenger to King Kuśa with a request to giving him Apratimā who would be his wife, and if Kuśa refused to do so, he should be ready for a fight. Jaṭhara further sent the message that Kuśa should inform him what he would like to do, otherwise Kuśa would have to submit to him (Jaṭhara). King Kuśa told his wife all about it. The queen shed tears and assured the king that she would cut off the body of Jaṭhara and would colour the earth with his blood; she further said that she was aware of innumerable sorts of magic and that Jaṭhara was insignificant to her. When Jaṭhara entered the harem of Kuśa he submitted to Queen Apratimā who placing her right leg on Jaṭhara's bosom and her left leg on his whiskers addressed him thus, "Oh, fool, have you not heard that a bee does not suck honey from a flowery creeper which is already being sucked by another bee? Don't you know that a forest elephant does not come forward to enjoy a lotus which is being enjoyed by another forest elephant?" King Jaṭhara prayed to the queen for protection and implored her to show mercy to him. Thereupon King Kuśa said to his wife Apratimā, "Oh, Queen, afford protection to this coward who is begging refuge, for to give protection to one who seeks shelter is the duty of a virtuous person".

Formerly a nāga king named Campaka was overpowered and subdued by an ahituṇḍika (snake-charmer). The nāga king knew that he could burn the ahituṇḍika (snake-charmer) who had lost his mantra and medicine, but he did not do so as he was pious.

Many persons named (1) Satyadharmavipulakīrti, (2) Sukīrti, (3) Lokābharan, (4) Vidyutprabha, (5) Indrateja, and others were helped to attain perfect enlightenment by the Lord Śākyasiṁha. Mahākāśyapa once said to Mahākātyāyana, "O, Jinaputra! Please relate the wonderful events of those who have passed from the ninth stage to the tenth one, have gone to Tuṣita heaven and desirous of human life, are born of mothers".

Mahākātyāyana replied, "One may be perfectly enlightened while in the womb, while about to be delivered or while being born".

The Bodhisattva, seeing the people of the world blinded by delusion, desired to be born on earth to save them, and thought within himself 'who is that lady who shall bear me, who has so much excellence that qualifies her to be my mother?' With this thought he saw Māyādevī possessed of this merit, in the harem of Śuddhodana and addressed the gods thus, 'I shall be born for the good of the world'. With folded hands, the gods said, 'We shall not be able to stay without you. We shall also live in the world to worship you'.

Thus the Bodhisattva entered into the womb of Māyādevī.

When the Bodhisattva stayed inside the mother's womb, he conversed with the gods. Celestial music regaled him in the womb. Marks of purity became visible on the countenance of his mother, Māyādevī, who informed Śuddhodana of her intention to pass her days in brahmacaryā, giving up malice and other faults. Celestial girls with flowers and garlands came to Māyādevī, paid her homage and said, "O, Queen, the Lord Bodhisattva resides in your womb". Conceiving the Bodhisattva the mother wore heavenly dress. Hundreds of thousands of heavenly girls conversed with her. She did not feel any pain due to child bearing. When she slept, heavenly girls waited upon her.

When Māyā's conception matured in the tenth

month, she made her desire of going to the Lumbini garden known to Śuddhodana and requested him to arrange for her conveyance. King Śuddhodana, according to Māyā's desire, made all arrangements and with his retinue took her to the pleasure garden. When Māyādevī caught hold of the branch of a Plakṣa tree and yawned, hundreds of thousands of nymphs came to her and said, 'To-day you will give birth to a son who will dissipate the fear of decrepitude and death'. Then Māyādevī brought forth the Bodhisattva with ease. Eight thousand gods in the guise of turbaned brahmin astrologers came there and sent word to the king through the warder. The gatekeeper spoke of the greatness of the persons in brahmin's dress and said, 'Methinks, gods have come in the guise of brahmins to see your son of great radiance'. The king gladly allowed them to come in. He saw them coming forward, got up from his seat with his company, and welcomed them with salutes. Then he seated them with great honour. Thereupon they explained to the king the necessity of their coming, "A son, with all signs, has been born unto you. We can read signs. We have come to see the child". The king showed them the child. They were very pleased and bowed down to the child who possessed all the signs of a great man.

The Bodhisattvas are not subject to passion in the Tuṣita heaven. Replying to the question about Rāhula's birth, Mahākātyāyana explained to Mahākāśyapa that the Bodhisattvas are not subject to passion for many a reason; Rāhula himself came down from the Tuṣita heaven, and entered into the womb of his mother Yaśodharā.

Then they described in verse the birth of the Bodhisattva. Then Mahākātyāyana said, "O, Mahākāśyapa, Bodhisattvas get five eyes such as (1) the human eye, (2) the divine eye, (3) the eye of wisdom, (4) the eye of universal knowledge, and (5) the eye of a Buddha. These five sorts of vision are their unique possession. When the Bodhisattvas acquire omniscience, they retain the power of seeing as far as they like because they have accumulated much merit. The human eye has unlimited quality. The ways of the perfectly enlightened one are beyond human knowledge. The human eye resembles eyes of other creatures in form and colour. The divine eye of the perfectly enlightened one is brighter, larger, and more distinct than the eyes of gods, Yakṣas, Rākṣasas, and terrestrial beings. It is engaged in rūpa (form) springing from the mind. The mental mastery over the ten forces is Dharmacakṣu, *i.e.*, the eye of universal knowledge. The ten forces are as follows:—The knowledge of proper and improper place is the first force; the knowledge of unknowable intelligence that moves in all directions is the second force; the knowledge of the world of different materials is the third force. The knowledge of different stages of adhimukti or will is the fourth force. The knowledge of the character of other persons is the fifth force. The force by which good or evil deeds are known is the sixth force. The knowledge of the annihilation of Kleśa is the seventh force. The knowledge of dhyāna-samāpatti, *i.e.*, the eight successive states induced by the ecstatic meditation is the eighth force. The knowledge of former states of existence is the ninth force. The tenth force is that by which the sacred divine eye is obtained and all evil passions (Kleśa) are annihilated".

There are eighteen kinds of Buddha-Dhamma (qualities of a Buddha)[1].

All the Exalted Buddhas are endowed with great virtue. The speech of the Exalted Buddhas has sixty qualities, *e.g.*, sweetness like that of music, sweet tune like that of a seven-stringed musical instrument, sweetness like the crackling of the swan, depth like that of thunder, the note of a cuckoo, the sound of a chariot, etc. They give instructions in the true law. They are truthful, speak of Dharma, Vinaya, etc. They are not attached to the worldly life although they are in this world. They are beyond old age, sorrow, death, etc. They are worshipped by all in this world.

[1] These are known as 18 āveṇikadharmas or āveṇiyadharmas. They are follows:—(1) seeing of all things past, (2) of all things future, (3) of all things present, (4) propriety of actions of the body, (5) of speech (6) of thought, (7) firmness of intention, (8) of memory (sati), (9) of concentration (samādhi), (10) of energy (viriya), (11) of emancipation (vimutti), (12) of wisdom (paññā), (13) freedom from fickleness or wantonness, (14) from noisiness, (15) from confusedness, (16) from hastiness, (17) from heedlessness, (18) from inconsiderateness (*vide* Kern's Manual of Indian Buddhism, p. 63).

In the Gṛdhrakuṭa mountain, in the assembly of five hundred persons who are controlled in their senses, instructions are given to the effect that all beings should desire to obtain Buddhahood.

Formerly there was a Cakravarttī king named Arcimāna. He had seven gems, *e.g.*, Cakraratna, hastiratna, aśvaratna, etc. He conquered the earth with her seas, mountains, and islands. He had a beautiful capital city named Dīpavatī. Sudīpā was his chief queen.

The Bodhisattvas are born either in brahmin or in Kṣatriya families. The family in which they take their birth is endowed with sixty aṅgas, *e.g.*, that family is full of many men and women, is famous, knows no fear, is full of enjoyments, firm in friendship, grateful to benefactors, and so forth.

Dīpaṅkara Bodhisattva

The Bodhisattva[1] Dīpaṅkara saw that Queen Sudīpā was immaculate and short-lived and that the span of her life was only ten months and seven nights more, so he made up his mind to be conceived by her, as one who would conceive the Bodhisattva would not be able to enjoy sensual pleasures. Then Sudīpā conceived Dīpaṅkara Bodhisattva. When the tenth month became full and complete, Sudīpā told her husband, King Arcimāna, that she would like to

[1] One who is destined to be a Buddha.

go to Padmavana. The king with his retinue took Sudīpā to Padmavana. As soon as the queen while roaming about by boat in the tank in this vana desired to descend from the boat, an island (dīpa) sprang up. The queen landed there and brought forth Dīpaṅkara Bodhisattva.

The queen Sudīpā with the Bodhisattva was brought to the capital city of Dīpavatī. The Suddhāvāsa devas came in disguise as brahmins and informed the king of the signs of greatness on the countenance of the newly-born child. Being requested by the king they named the boy, Dīpaṅkara. When Dīpaṅkara became a youth the king built three palaces for the enjoyment of the prince. The Bodhisattva went to Padmavana for enjoyment in the tank, there were good many objects of enjoyment but the Bodhisattva was not attached to them. He became indifferent to the world and practised samādhi or self-concentration to acquire divine insight. With a concentrated mind in the middle watch of the night he began to recollect his former births. After many years, Dīpaṅkara acquired perfect enlightenment and in order to do good to the world he came to Dīpavatī with eighty thousand bhikkhus to show favour to his father, Arcimāna and relatives. King Arcimāna approached to welcome him and brought him to Dīpavati. At this time being charmed by the influence of Dīpaṅkara, a Vedic student, named Megha, became his disciple. Megha's class mate, named Meghadatta, who heard of Dīpaṅkara, told Megha that he would not be able to follow him as he had not then completed the study of the Vedas. Later, Meghadatta being enamoured of another man's wife killed his preventive mother and disclosed the facts of matricide to his mistress who was alarmed to hear of this and forbade him to come to her. Meghadatta then became attached to his step-mother and at her instance killed his father.

All his relatives knowing everything shunned his company. Then he removed to a different place. Once upon a time a bhikkhu who knew about the family of his father went for alms to the spot where Meghadatta had been staying. He was killed by the latter who feared that he might divulge every thing concerning his character. In consequence of all these sinful deeds Meghadatta was reborn in hell.

When the Lord Śākyamuni after attaining perfect enlightenment, was turning the wheel of law, this Meghadatta was living as a timiṅgila (a fabulous fish of an enormous size) in the Ocean. When a householder named Thapakarṇi was making a voyage, this fish was about to swallow him up but Thapakarṇi was saved by the Buddha. The fish, as soon as it heard of the name of the Buddha, remembered, at once, all about Dīpaṅkara. By thinking about the Buddha at the end of life it was reborn in a brahman's family at Śrāvastī. When he grew up, he became a religious mendicant and disciple of the Bodhisattva.

Maṅgala Buddha

After the Exalted Buddha, there arose another Exalted Buddha named Maṅgala. The span of his life was hundred thousand crores of years. He had three congregations of disciples. The first congregation had hundred thousand crores of disciples; the second, ninety crores of disciples; and the third, eighty crores of disciples. Sudeva and Dharmadeva were two principal disciples and there were also two chief female disciples named Śivatī and Aśokā. Maṅgala's father was a Kṣatriya king and his mother was named 'Śrī'.

There lived in Kuṇḍalā near the Himalayas, a Yakṣī (ogress) who had many sons who were sent to Vaiśālī to destroy the vitality of the people. The Vaiśalians gradually began to die of disease and were eager to find out one who would be able to drive away the disease. They thought about the matter and brought many notable persons such as Kāśyapapūraṇa but in vain. They sent a deputation headed by Tomara, a Licchavi chief of power and position....and at the same time of great learning, to Rājagṛha to bring the Exalted One to their city. Tomara went to Rājagṛha, fell down at the feet of the Master, and sought his help with supplications, but he was asked to apply to King Śreṇika Bimbisāra who insisted on the condition that the Licchavis must welcome the Buddha at the border of their own dominions and that he himself would follow the Great Teacher to the boundaries of his own territory. To this, the Licchavis readily assented and Bimbisāra secured the consent of the Buddha to save the Licchavis from the decimating disease.

The Magadhan king, to impress the Licchavis with an idea of his power and opulence, had the road all the way from Rājagṛha to the Ganges, which formed the boundary between the two dominions, levelled, rendered clean like the palm of the hand, decorated with flags, garlands, and richly embroidered cloth; besides, the whole road was watered, flowers were freely scattered upon it and the smoke of rich incense perfumed its whole length. He himself followed the Enlightened One with his whole court and numerous retinue. The Licchavis both the Abhyantara Vaiśālakas, the Vaiśāli-cockneys proper, living within the walls of the city and the Bāhira-Vaiśālakas, the people living in the outer town, the suburbs and surroundings—came in all their splendour and magnificence, in all the glory of their dazzling, garments, blue, purple, green, yellow, brown, and crimson; their appearance, as they approached was so splendid and ravishing that even the Great Buddha was impressed with the sight and said addressing the monks, "Bhikkhus, you have never beheld before the Trayastiṁsa gods, as they go out of their city, Sudarsanā, to the garden. Behold now the Licchavis of Vaiśālī who equal those gods in their prosperity and splendour. Look at the Licchavis with their elephants, with umbrellas of gold, their gold-covered litters, their chariots decorated with gold. See how they all come, both the young and the aged as also those of middle age, all with ornaments on, with garments dyed crimson with lac and advancing with various beautiful movements". The Licchavis of Vaiśālī decorated the road from the Ganges to Vaiśālī with a magnificence that left the preparations made by the Magadhan king far behind, they provided for the comfort of the Exalted One and the congregation of monks on a still more lavish scale. As soon as the Enlightened One crossed over to the northern side of the river and stepped on the Licchavi soil, all malign influences that had hung over the country and were making a havoc among the people, vanished, and the sick and the suffering were restored to health. The Licchavis received him with all honour and reverence and guided him to their city, by easy stages with all the comfort and convenience that they were able to provide for him. Entering the city, the Enlightened One uttered the Svastyayanagāthā, the song of welfare, or according to the Pāli scriptures, the Ratana Sutta, he was asked as to whether he would live among the people of inner Vaiśālī or of outer Vaiśālī. The Exalted One would not live among either of them. but he accepted the invitation of Bhagavatī Gośṛṅgi in the Mahāvana, the great forest, extending from their city far away to the north.

The Licchavis who wished that the Exalted One would be induced to live in their city, built the Kuṭāgārasālā, the peaked monastery, for him in the forest and paid their respects to him there. They offered it to him and the Buddhist congregation and he permitted the bhikkhus to reside there. One day, the Licchavis on coming to the Mahāvana learnt that the Exalted One had repaired to the Cāpāla caitya for spending the day; they proceeded there and presented it to him and the congregation of the Śrāvakas or Buddhist monks.

Similarly finding the Exalted One spending the day at the Saptāmra-caitya, the Bahuputra-caitya, the Gautama-caitya, the Kapinhya-caitya, and the Markaṭa-harda-tīra-caitya,[1] the Licchavis made a gift of all these places of worship to the Exalted One and the Buddhist Church. Next the courtesan, (gaṇikā) Āmrapālī, made a gift of her extensive mango-grove to the congregation and similarly Bālikā made over Bālikā chavi.

Once upon a time the Buddha Gautama with a larger number of bhikkhus was staying at *Marakanda* in the kingdom of Kośala. In the evening the Blessed One coming out of the hermitage looked around, went up and down, and laughed a

---

[1] Cf. Mahāparinibbāṇa Sutta of the Dīgha Nikāya.

little. Ānanda noticing this came to the bhikkhus and said thus, "The Blessed One has laughed. The Exalted Buddha does not laugh where there is no reason for laughing. We shall ask the Blessed One about the cause of his laughter". The bhikkhus agreed to do so and went with Ānanda to the Blessed One and asked him about the cause of his laughter. The Blessed One replied thus, "O, Ānanda, the world which is before you, is the abode of Kāśyapa, is the place where Kāśyapa walked up and down. It is in this world that three Tathāgatas dwelt, namely, Kakucchanda Kanakamuni, and Kāśyapa." Hearing this, Ānanda saluted the Buddha and asked him to sit in the place as it would then be connected with the incidents in the life of the four Tathāgatas. Ānanda and other Bhikkhus saluted the Blessed One and sat on one side. The Blessed One asked Ānanda, "O, Ānanda! Are you willing to listen to the religious discourse in connection with the former abodes of the Tathāgata?" Ānanda replied, "O, Blessed One, This is the time to listen to the religious discourse". The Blessed One related the following story: "O, Ānanda"! At the time of Kāśyapa Buddha, there was a Brahmin village named Verudiṅga. There lived a potter named Ghaṭikāra. He was a great devotee of Kāśyapa. He had a play-mate who was also a brahmin's son, named Jyotipāla. Once the Blessed One came to this Verudiṅga village with his disciples. Ghaṭikāra heard of this and he also informed Jyotipāla of this and asked him to go with him to see Kāśyapa. But Jyotipāla did not give his consent. Ghaṭikāra thought of various means of bringing Jyotipāla to the Buddha. Ghaṭikāra took Jyotipāla to a tank not far from the place where Kāśyapa was, with the intention of bathing in the tank. They bathed in the tank and Ghaṭikāra afterwards asked Jyotipāla to go to that part of the neighbouring forest where Kāśyapa Buddha was dwelling. Jyotipāla refused to do so but Ghaṭikāra holding him by the neck said thus, "He lives in the forest, let us go to him and worship him". Jyotipāla again refused to do so and left Ghaṭikāra. Ghaṭikāra then followed him, caught hold of the hair of his hand, and made special requests to go to Kāśyapa. Jyotipāla thought thus, "Ghaṭikāra, though he is of low birth, has caught hold of the hair of my hand not for a slight reason. It is better to comply with his request". Jyotipāla then went to Kāśyapa with Ghaṭikāra and after saluting him they sat on one side. Ghaṭikāra requested the Buddha to give some instructions to his companion, a brahmin's son. The Blessed One instructed Jyotipāla in the three refuges and five precepts. Jyotipāla said to the Blessed One, "I cannot follow the five precepts as I have got to kill a person". Being questioned by the Blessed One he answered thus, "This Ghaṭikāra has caught hold of my hair after my bath". The Blessed One pacified him by his religious instructions. Jyotipāla then promised to accept the five precepts, and asked Ghaṭikāra, "Have you properly realised religious instructions of the Blessed One?" Ghaṭikāra answered in the affirmative. Jyotipāla then questioned him, "It is proper for you to accept renunciation". Ghaṭikāra replied, "I am the only support of my parents and it is for this reason that I cannot accept ordination from the Blessed One".

Then Jyotipāla began to hate the world and he told Ghaṭikāra to go to the Blessed One for ordination. At the command of the Blessed One the bhikkhus gave him ordination.

Once upon a time Kāśyapa was dwelling at Ṛṣipatana Mṛgadāva (Sārnāth at Benares). As soon as King Kṛki heard the news, he sent a person to the Blessed One to request him to accept invitation to his palace which the Buddha Kāśyapa did.

The Blessed One was informed thus, "King Kṛki spent the night in making ready the food for the Blessed One and reminds the Blessed One of the invitation". The Buddha Kāśyapa went to the royal residence at Benares with his disciples to take his food at the palace of king Kṛki. The King saw him from a distance and saluted him. A new palace was built at the royal city unused by the Śramaṇas and the Brāhmaṇas, and it was at this palace that Kāśyapa took his residence. The King brought food for the Buddha at this palace. The king offered the food to the Buddha with his own hand and while the Blessed

One was taking rest, he bowed to his feet. He requested the Buddha to spend the rainy season at Benares and promised to build an ārāma (hermitage), thousand kuṭāgāras, streets, etc. But when the Blessed One did not comply with his request, the king gave vent to his grief and afterwards implored him thus, "O, the Blessed One! Have you got a disciple like unto me?" The Blessed one replied, "I have a better disciple than you and he is the potter, named Ghaṭikāra of the village of Veruḍiṅga". Ghaṭikāra strictly followed the ten precepts throughout his life. He never dug new land. He made earthen pots with the earth taken from the land damaged by water or by ants and placed them on the cross-way to be taken away by the person who liked them and he was the only support of his old parents. Once the Blessed One went to Veruḍiṅga and came to the house of the potter to take food when he was not at home, his blind parents offered soup and cooked rice to the Blessed One. The potter afterwards returned home and was informed of the arrival of the Buddha by his parents and became very much pleased. On another occasion, grass was needed to cover up the forest hut of the Tathāgata, and the old parents of the potter were told by the bhikkhus that they were in need of grass for covering the newly-built hut. Thereupon the bhikkhus were permitted to take the grass and were further told that they might regard it as their own. The potter was not then at home. He afterwards returned and was informed of the taking of grass by the bhikkhus and became very much pleased. After hearing all this, King Kṛki thought that the Blessed One was dwelling in his kingdom. The Buddha Kāśyapa then went away after giving religious instructions to the king.

Jyotipāla made up his mind to become an Exalted Buddha like Kāśyapa for the good of the world. Kāśyapa came to know of the determination of Jyotipāla and afterwards told him that he would surely become the Exalted Buddha. Bhikkhu Jyotipala offered a golden stool to the Buddha Kāśyapa and thought within himself, "Like Kāśyapa, I shall attain perfect enlightenment and do good to the world. Then gods and men will respectfully listen to my words. I shall free myself and free others! Being consoled, I shall console others! Abstained from worldly affairs I shall cause people to follow my example, I shall cause the people to be established in the sublime dharma, I shall light the torch of Dharma, sound the drum of Dharma, hoist the flag of Dharma, and blow the conch of Dharma. I shall free the persons suffering in the six kinds of hell, *viz.*, Sañjīva, Kālasūtra, Saṅghāta, Raurava, Mahāraurava, and Avīci[1]. I shall give instructions to people in Vinaya as the Buddha Kāśyapa is at present doing".

[1] For detailed accounts of these hells, *vide* my book "Heaven and Hell in Buddhist Perspective".

CHAPTER II

Gautama, the Buddha

Kalyāna was the son of King Sammata. Kalyāna begot Rava. Rava begot Uposadha whose son was King Māndhāta. King Māndhāta had many thousands of sons and grandsons. Later on, Sujāta became king of the Ikṣākus, in the city of Sāketa. The Ikṣāku king, Sujāta, had five sons, Opura, Nipura, Karakaṇḍaka, Ulkāmukha, and Hastikaśīrṣa, and he had five daughters, Suddhā, Vimalā, Vijitā, Jalā, Jalī; Sujāta had another son, Jenta by name, born of a concubine, named Jentī, who served the king with the devotion of a married wife. Sujāta became pleased with her and said to her, "Jentī, I will offer you a boon, whatever boon you pray for, I will grant it". She said, "O, king! Let me first consult my parents before I pray for a boon to your Lordship". She then asked her parents who told her to pray for a village. But a shrewd Buddhist nun counselled her thus, "Well, Jentī, you are a concubine. Your son will not inherit any property of his father, what to speak of a kingdom. The five legitimate sons of the king will inherit their paternal kingdom as well as other things. You are promised a boon by King Sujāta who is a man of word. So pray for the exile of the five princes and the appointment of your son, Jenta, as successor to the throne. After the death of the king, your son will be king of the great city of Sāketa and every thing will be yours". Jenti acted up to the advice of the nun. King Sujāta became much agitated in mind owing to the affection for those princes. But afraid of the sin of the breach of promise he granted the boon. The gift of the boon that with the exile of the five princes, the prince Jenta, son of the concubine, was to be installed as heir-apparent, was heard by the people of towns and villages. Then the people appreciating the noble qualities of the five princes became alarmed and said, "Wherever the princes will go, we shall follow them". King Sujāta came to know that many people of Sāketa were going to the place of exile along with the princes and he ordered that elephants, horses, chariots, carriages, palanquins, or, cars, or oxen or buffaloes or goats or sheep, etc., would be given to those who would follow the princes. Under royal orders the royal treasury was open to all the followers of the princes who got every thing that they asked for. The five princes along with many thousands of citizens and thousands of chariots and carriages, went out of the city of Sāketa towards the north. They were cordially received by the king of Kāśī-Kośala. The princes were virtuous, well-reputed, peaceful, and good companions. All the people of Kāśī-Kośala were charmed with the qualities of their head and heart. The king of Kāśī-Kośala marked his peoples' attachment to the princes and thought that this might result in his own destruction and in the enthronement of the princes. Thereupon he became envious and drove out the princes from his kingdom. At the foot of the Himalayas, there lived a sage, Kapila, who was possessed of five kinds of supernatural knowledge and had attained the four kinds of meditation. He was strong and noble in mind. His hermitage was vast and charming. It had fruits and flowers and it was adorned with good many plants and with a dense forest known as Śākoṭavana. The princes went to this forest and settled there. Traders used to come here from Kāśī and Kośala. When asked by the people as to whence they had come, the traders replied that they had come from a certain part of the forest called Sākoṭavana. The people of Sāketa too used to visit the Sākoṭavana. Lest there should be adulteration of blood in their clan, they married girls of their own clan and even their own sisters. King Sujāta asked his ministers as to the whereabouts of the princes. The ministers told the king that the princes had settled in the Sākoṭavana at the foot of the Himalayas. Then the king asked the ministers, "Wherefrom did they bring their wives?" They replied, "It was heard that for the fear of a mixture of blood in them, they accepted their wives from among their own sisters by the same mother so that there might not be any contamination in their own race". The purohitas and the learned brahmins were then asked by king Sujāta whether such a custom was permissible. They replied, "Yes, O king, that can be done, laws permit it". Hearing this, the king being pleased named them as the Śākyas. Sometime after, the princes marked the increase in the population of Sākoṭavana and thought of building another town. They then came to the sage Kapila. Saluting him they said, "If your grace permit, we may build a city here to be called Kapilavastu after your name". The sage replied, "I can permit it if you make this hermitage a royal residence and then build a city". The princes promised to carry out his wishes. The hermitage was then given to them by the sage. The princes built a city after making the hermitage of the sage a royal residence. As the hermitage was given by Kapila the sage, it was known by the name of Kapilavastu which was prosperous, wealthy, peaceful, where alms were easily obtainable, where many people lived with their own families, being happy. The people of Kapilavastu were fond of trade and commerce. They were social and took part in festivities.

Of these five princes, Opura, Nipura, Karakaṇḍaka, Ulkāmukha, Hastikaśirṣa, Opura was the eldest prince. He was elected king of Kapilavastu. Nipura was the son of king Opura and Karakaṇḍaka was the son of King Nipura. Ulkāmukha [1]

---

[1] Cf. Dīpavaṁsa and Mahāvaṁsa. Please refer to Dulva, the Tibetan translation of the Vinaya of the Sarvāstivadins.

was the son of king Karakaṇḍaka. Hastikaśīrṣa was the son of Ulkāmukha. Sinhahanu was the son of Hastikaśirṣa. King Sinhahanu had four sons: Suddhodana, Dhautodana, Śuklodana, Amritodana,[1] and a daughter, named Amṛtā.

A daughter of a certain Śākya noble who was handsome and endowed with all good qualities, was attacked with leprosy. The physicians treated her in vain, the disease being incurable. They prescribed ointments and laxative medicines for her. Sores appeared all over the body. The people began to hate her. She was taken by all the brothers in a palanquin to a spot close to the Himalayas. They dug out a subterranean room and she was left there with abundance of food and water. They put planks to block the path leading to the interior of the cave and the doors were closed and they put a big heap of dust in front of the cave and then they returned to Kapilavastu. Living in that stuffy room in the heat of the cave, she was cured of leprosy. Her body became altogether soreless and she regained her former beauty. A tiger got human smell, came towards the cave, and began to throw off the heap of dust. Not far from the cave lived a royal sage, named Kola, who was possessed of five supernatural knowledges and had attained the four kinds of meditation. His hermitage was full of vegetables,

---

[1] Cf. the Mahāvaṁsa account.

flowers, and fruits. It was very charming. The sage while wandering hither and thither in the vicinity of the hermitage, came to the cave where the Śākya girl lived. The tiger threw off the heap of dust with its legs, leaving only the plank. The tiger was seen by the sage who compelled it to leave that spot and go away. As the sage saw the tiger throwing off the dust, curiosity arose in his mind. Then the plank having been removed by the sage, the door of the cave was opened. The Śākya girl was seen in all her great beauty. The sage asked, "Well lady, who are you?" She replied, "I am the daughter of a certain Śākya noble of Kapilavastu. Having fallen a victim to leprosy, I have been left here to spend the rest of my life". Seeing the exquisite beauty of the Śākya girl he became very much attached to her. Coming in contact with the Śākya girl, the sage lost the power of meditation and his supernatural knowledge. He then went to the hermitage along with the Śākya girl who lived in the hermitage with the sage Kola. Sixteen pairs of twin sons were born to them. Thirty-two sons of the sage, when they grew up, were sent to Kapilavastu by their mother who said to them thus, "Sons, go to the city of Kapilavastu where live my father and your maternal grandfather. There the sons of such and such persons are your maternal uncles and they are Śākya nobles and your relations. They will provide you with means to maintain yourselves". She trained them thus in the manners of the Śākyas, "You will approach a Śākya gentleman in this way. This is the proper way to salute. In this way you should sit down". Having trained them in the manners of the Śākyas, they were allowed to go. They saluted their parents, went round them, and then went away. In course of time they reached Kapilavastu. They entered Kapilavastu and impressed all with their beautiful appearance. The vast crowd seeing the sons of the sage received them and said, "These sons of the sage are beautiful and have plaited hairs". They went to the Mote-Hall of the Śākyas surrounded by a vast crowd. Five hundred Śākyas assembled in the Mote-Hall for some business. They approached the Śākya assembly in the way they were taught by their mother. The Śākya assembly became astonished to see the Śākya manners in them. The Śākya assembly asked the sons of the sage thus, "Wherefrom do you come?" As instructed they answered thus, "We are sons of Kola, the royal sage who has his hermitage somewhere at the foot of the Himalayas. Our mother is the daughter of a certain Śākya noble". Hearing them, the Śākyas became pleased. Their maternal grandfather who was one of the leading Śākyas and whose lineage was noble, was still alive. The royal sage Kola gave his eldest son the kingdom of Benares and he went out of the kingdom for ordination. The Śākyas were then very glad to learn that they were born of the royal sage and not of persons of inferior rank. They said, "They must also be Śākyas. They belong to the same caste to which we belong. Let them be given Śākya brides, cultivable lands, and villages". As the princes were born of the sage Kola, they were known as Koliyas.

The Śākyas had a country named Devadaha where a chief of the Śākyas named Subhuti married a Koliya girl who brought forth seven daughters, namely, Māyā,[1] Mahāmāyā, Atimāyā, Anantamāyā, Cūliyā, Kolīsovā, and Mahāprajāpatī. We have already told that the Śākya king, Sinhahanu, had four sons among whom Śuddhodana was one. On the death of King Sinhahanu, Śuddhodana ascended the throne and he expressed his desire to his ministers to marry a beautiful girl. The ministers sent some brahmins conversant with the study of signs on the person of human being, in quest of a beautiful girl. The brahmins came to Devadaha and selected Māyā, one of the daughters of Subhuti. King Śuddhodana sent a message to Subhuti to give his daughter Māyā in marriage to him. Subhuti replied that he had six other daughters who were older in age than Māyā and after giving them in marriage he would be able to offer his seventh daughter to him, and Śuddho-

---

1 Cf. Spence Hardy's Manual of Buddhism, p. 125 foll.

dana asked for the hands of the seven maids. In compliance with his request Subhuti offered his seven daughters who were brought to Kapilavastu from Devadaha by Śuddhodana. Among the seven daughters, Māyā and Mahāprajāpatī were kept in Śuddhodana's harem and the remaining five were given to his five brothers. The Buddha Gautama was the son of Queen Māyā.

Gautama's early life

While descending from the Tuṣita heaven, the Bodhisattva took into consideration the proper time, country, continent, and family to be born in. The Bodhisattva is generally born either in a brahmin family when the brahmins are supreme or in a Kṣatriya family when the Kṣatriyas attain superiority. The family, which the Bodhisattva would be born in, should have sixty well-known attributes. A thousand gods brought four great kings to the Tuṣita heaven during the Bodhisattva's descent, and said to one of them, *viz.*, Bimbisāra, "Be born in Rājagṛha. If you follow righteousness, then others will do so". Thus Abhaya, Sārthavāha, and other great brahmins and householders were born. The gods said to another king (Udayana, king of the Vatsas), "Be born in Kauśāmbī. If you follow rules of discipline or humility then great men will do so". The householder, Ghośila, and other great Kṣatriyas and householders observed rules of discipline. Thousands of devaputras (sons of gods) were born in different families of Brahmans, Kṣatriyas, and householders in the sixteen great countries (mahājanapadas) to be the companions of the Lord. The Bodhisattva cogitated about the persons fit to be his parents. He thought of Śuddhodana as a worthy father. He then thought of the mother who should bear him. He resolved to be born in the womb of a mother who is cheerful, kulin (of good family), of pure body, and of short life, *i.e.*, the span of her life should be ten months and seven days only. The mother who conceives Bodhisattva dies generally within seven days from the date of delivery. Thinking of such a mother, Bodhisattva saw that the chief queen of Śuddhodana was endowed with the requisite qualities. He then considered her worthy to be his mother. The Bodhisattva informed the Devasaṁgha of his intention. The Devasaṁgha[1] approved this heartily and promised to descend to earth for the benefit of mankind. The Assembly of gods began to sing hymns. While such discussions were going on in Tuṣita heaven, King Śuddhodana at the request of his chief queen Māyā, brought her to the well-decorated palace named Dhṛtarāṣtra. The queen lay on her right side. Gods saw her sleeping and came down to the top of the palace. They did obeisance to her with folded hands. Daughters of gods with holy garlands came there to see the Jina's mother and from heaven they began to shower flowers. All sides of the firmament were

[1] It means an assembly of gods.

protected by monsters, serpents, yakṣas, and gandharvas. Desired by gods, the Lord came down to earth. At this time, Māyā dreamt that an elephant, with good looks, a red head, and six tusks and of slow movement entered into her womb. The Bodhisattvas are generally conceived on the full-moon night with the predominating star, Puṣyā. The Bodhisattva created such a light as lit up the whole Buddha world. The Bodhisattva descended and the earth quaked, but not a being was injured. Indra and the other gods began to guard the Lord in the mother's womb. The next morning Māyādevī told her husband every thing about her dream. The king asked the fortune-tellers about the significance of this dream. They said, "O Lord! A son of great goddess will be born with thirty-two signs. If this child be a householder, he will be a rājcakravarttī, if the child enter into a monastic order he will be the leader of the world". Conceiving a Bodhisattva, the mother feels happiness in every work. She does not feel any pain resembling that of being pierced with weapon. Poison, fire, and thunder cannot injure her. Daughters of gods serve the mother. She gets heavenly cloth, ornament, perfumes, garlands, and pastes and is respected by the members of the family. The Bodhisattva while in mother's womb is not smeared with biles, phlegm, and blood. His body is clean and washed. The Bodhisattva in mother's womb can see the mother who also can see the child like a golden

(Copyright, Archæological Survey of India)

Dream of Queen Māyā

idol. Gods come twice a day to hear of the happy day and the happy night. The Bodhisattva too cheers them up by raising his right arm. Thousands and thousands of nymphs dance and sing songs before the mother of the Bodhisattva. Thousands of heavenly daughters talk with her and fan her while asleep with a cluster of coral trees (mandāra). On the completion of ten months the mother bearing Bodhisattva is delivered.

The Śākya Subhuti sent word to the king that the chief queen should go to her parent's residence for delivery. The king consented to the queen's departure. On the way, the royal party arrived at the Lumbini garden which was full of sweet-smelling flowers. The air was scented by the leaves of the Tamāla tree, and filled with the perfume of aguru and incense.

Gods and their daughters repaired to the Lumbini garden with scented garlands.

Māyādevi with her friends came to the garden in a chariot. Thousands of country-girls and villagers stood there with folded hands to wait upon her. The mother bearing a Bodhisattva did not lie down or sit to give birth to child. She stood and gave birth to the child. She felt no pain during delivery. The Bodhisattva appeared on the right side. While born, he took seven steps and with a smiling face he looked around. Heavenly flowers were showered upon him from the sky. First the gods, then human beings took him on their lap.

The world became bright. There were two showers of water hot and cold for Bodhisattva's bath. Sons of gods held in the sky umbrella bedecked with precious jewels.

By the influence of Sugata,[1] the mother remained uninjured. Her womb acquired its original form. Thousand sons of gods and nymphs came there to worship the Bodhisattva. With the birth of Bodhisattva there were born in Śākya family five hundred male children foremost of whom was the beautiful Nanda, five hundred female children foremost of whom was Yaśodharā, the same number of servants, the first of whom was Chandaka, the same number of horses, Kaṇṭhaka heading the list, the same number of elephants the foremost was Candana, and the like number of divine treasures. King Śuddhodana ordered his men to bring Māyādevī to Kapilavastu. Viśvakarmā built a palanquin set with jewels. Four great kings came there to carry the palanquin. The Bodhisattva with Māyā got into the palanquin. Mahābrahmā, the lord, drove away the crowd. King Śuddhodana sent the child to gods to show respects to Abhayādevī. Abhayādevī herself bowed down to the prince. With the birth of the prince, King Śuddhodana was successful in every thing, hence the prince was called 'Sarvārthasiddha'. The prince entered the palace. King asked his priest to find out brahmins who were

---

[1] It is an epithet of the Buddha Gautama. It means a Blessed One.

skilful in studying signs. The eight hundred sons of gods came to the palace as brahmans skilful in reading signs. The king paid due respects to them. They declared, "The prince has thirty-two signs". In the Vindhya hills, there lived with five hundred disciples a sage named Asita versed in the Vedas. He noticed an earthquake, flower-rain, and other miracles of the like, sat in meditation and learnt that the Bodhisattva had been born. He came to Kapilavastu to see the Buddha and was given a respectful ovation. Sage Asita shed tears to see the prince. Questioned by the king, the sage said, "I hear this prince will be Rājcakravarttī, but he would not be so, I think. He will be a Buddha. I am an old man. I shall not live so long. I shed tears in sorrow as I shall not have the opportunity of hearing Buddha's religious counsels".

Once the king went to the garden with the prince and other members of the family. The prince noticed ploughing. A snake and a frog were dug out by the plough. The prince threw away the snake that was ready to devour the frog. This caused him to feel pain of body and life. He at once began to brood over the question of the renunciation of the world. He sat under the shade of a Jambu tree. The shade did not move with the movement of the Sun. The king searched for the prince at meal time. All quarters were searched and the prince was found under the shade of the Jambu tree. The king was informed of it. He came there, found him in this plight and bowed down to him. The king thought if the prince be meditative as he was at the time, then the words of the sage Asita would turn out to be true; he got a large harem built for the prince to keep him in his house. He had various aśokabhāṇḍa built and made a declaration throughout his kingdom that the prince would distribute ornaments amongst girls. Let every girl come to the royal garden. Thousands of girls came to the royal garden and received ornaments. Yaśodharā, daughter of a Śākya named Mahānāma, came there well-decorated. Yaśodharā did not come close to the prince through bashfulness.

On his attainment of Buddha-hood, the lord was asked by the bhikkhus the reason for this. The Lord said that it was not merely at this birth but in previous births as well that she did so.

Buddha's Renunciation and religious life

While at Śrāvastī, the Lord Buddha once said to the bhikkhus, "I was a very beautiful boy. My father, Śuddhodana, had three palaces built for me, where I was to reside during cold season (hemanta), the summer, and the rains for my sport, dalliance, and walk. In these palaces, there were gabled halls (Kuṭāgāras) with a covered porch and scented with incense, covered with silk and satin cloth and strewn with flowers. In the halls, there were various bedsteads of gold, and silver set with precious stones, many pillows smelling sweet scent like agurucandana; various fine cloths, garlands of campaka flowers; there was provision for dancing and singing, musical instruments, trumpets; beautiful ladies. Horses, elephants, and various other vehicles and saddle made of lion skin, various umbrellas and all other articles of luxury were collected. There were gardens on all sides, and round the gardens, lotus lakes, and other lakes were dug out. High and big palaces were built. These were provided for my pleasure. But living in a house seemed to me to be confinement. I thought that salvation lay in becoming a religious mendicant. It was not possible to practise brahmacaryā at home. So I became a religious mendicant. I caused my parents to weep, renounced the imperial throne, accepted the life of a mendicant, and proceeded towards Vaiśālī.

In Vaiśālī there was a brahmin named Ārāḍa Kālāma who instructed his three hundred disciples on Dharma. He used to say to Śrāvakas[1] and brāhmaṇas, 'See and Sacrifice' (paśyatha, paśyatha, prajahatha, prajahatha). The disciples too used to say, 'we are seeing and sacrificing'. I became a disciple of Ārāḍa-Kālāma. In a very short time, I found out that the dharma taught by Ārāḍa Kālāma could not bring out an end to all suffering. Then with a view to acquire something higher, I proceeded towards Rājagṛha. On arriving there, I heard of Udrakārāmaputra who used to instruct seven hundred disciples on dharma.

---

[1] It means disciples. In Pali it is sāvakas.

I became his disciple. By dint of perseverance, I learnt dharma in a very short time and realised that his dharma too was incapable of putting an end to misery. Then I went to Gayā.

While roaming on the Gayāśirṣa mountain three unheard of analogies crossed my mind.

The first simile:—As a man desirous of getting light cannot produce fire by rubbing one wet wood against another wet wood inside water, so a person with passionate thoughts does not become respectful to one who is with passionate mind and body. He suffers misery only. He cannot acquire knowledge.

Second simile:—As a man desirous of getting light cannot produce fire by rubbing one wet wood against another wet wood on the ground, so a person with a passionate mind does not become respectful to one who is free from passion. He suffers only and cannot acquire knowledge.

Third simile:—As a man desirous of getting light can produce fire by rubbing one dry wood against another dry wood on the ground, so a passionate man becomes modest to one who endures severe physical pain and whose mind and body are free from passion. He can acquire knowledge.

I thought I too should go on with mind free from desire and body free from passion. The passionate would be humble to me. I should endure severe physical pain. I should be able to acquire the best knowledge for a man.

Thus resolved I proceeded towards Uruvilva.

There I saw nicely-looking roots, pleasing lakes, plain grounds, and the sanctifying water of the Nairañjanā river. I was delighted. There I began to practise austerity. I suppressed my body by mind in such a way that perspiration came out of my face and forehead and fell on the ground. Sweat streamed down the outskirts of my cloth.

I began to practise Āsphānaka meditation. I stopped breath through mouth and nose. I heard inside my ears a great sound like blacksmith's pitcher. I confined the air in the holes of my ear. This air struck my brain like the sharp instrument of the butcher striking the head of an ox.

I ate only one plum. My body became so lean that ribs could be counted, the spinal cord could be seen, eyes sank to their sockets, the head became dry, the colour of the body became black. Somebody became accomplished by living on rice only. I too began to eat rice. Body became lean as before. Depending on Sesamum only, my body became lean as before. I stopped that for ever and my body became more lean. Then it struck me that this was the utmost limit to be reached by penance; nothing further than this could be attained. Perfect knowledge was not to be acquired through this path. I thought that the delightful first penance which I acquired underneath the cold shadow of Jambu tree from sin and desire just before the retirement of the world, is the best road to the acquisition of knowledge.

Such a penance was not possible for a weak man in starvation. Then I began to take juice of pulse.[1]

My appetite increased. I got strength. I took honey and rice boiled in milk, (*i.e.*, pāyasa) and came to the banks of the Nairañjanā river. My body became cold after a bath in Nairañjanā. I took some grass from a grass cutter, prepared a cushion before the Bodhi tree which I circumambulated and I took my seat there. I attained the first stage of meditation and roamed about with a mind free from passion and sin. On the cessation of Sabitarkavicāra (determination of truth after discussion), mind got delighted. The second stage of meditation was reached. Then embracing renunciation, I neglected delight (prīti) and attained the third stage. Pleasure and pain came to an end. Affection and affliction disappeared. The fourth stage, *viz.*, that of sukha, upekkhā, and smriti, was reached. Then I could see every thing with spiritual eyes. I found certain people going to hell in consequence of their evil deeds and others to heaven by virtue of good deeds. Then I remembered the events of my past life. Events of hundreds of my previous births were vivid. At the end of the night, at sunrise, all that were worthy to be known, got and understood, came to my knowledge. I acquired Perfect Enlightenment (Samyaksambodhi).

---

1 Mug, Kulattha, and Harenuka.

Śuddhodana saw in a dream an elephant bedecked with gems, standing on the road in the midst of the city. Seeing this, he laughed and wept in his dream; his body trembled and suffered a scorching pain. The lokapālas asked the King not to be afraid and explained to him the significance of this dream. "In order to impart knowledge to many people", they said, "a son has been born to you, endowed with various qualities. He will give up the kingdom. Worldly miseries will then disappear. This is the meaning of your laugh in the dream. The effect of your crying in the dream will be that your son will attain jinahood, he will obtain eternal bliss, and conquer all the enemies".

The Buddha's mother's sister, too, saw in a dream a white coloured bullock running in the city of Kapilavastu making a pleasing sound. The king of the gods came and told her that the chief of men, Sarvārthasiddha, will leave this world and will obtain Nirvāṇa.

Yaśodharā saw in a dream a heavy shower of rain in the royal family and as the result of that shower, every body was refreshed. Brahmā came and told her that the Buddha would give happiness to all people by his instruction and he would preach the incomparable Dharma.

The Bodhisattva dreamt five great dreams. In the first dream, he saw that this world was his bed, the mount Sumeru was his pillow, and his left hand was on the eastern ocean while his right hand was on the western ocean, and his feet were on the southern ocean. In consequence of this great dream, he attained perfect enlightenment. In the second dream, he saw that a grass named Khīrikā originated from his belly which spread all over the sky.

The Buddha after having acquired the supreme knowledge turned the Wheel of Law at Ṛṣipatana Mṛgadāva in Benares. That is to say, he preached the four noble truths, suffering, origin of suffering, cessation of suffering, and the path leading to the cessation of suffering. Not a śramaṇa, brāhmaṇa, or deva, or māra, or any other person did turn the wheel of such a dharma. This dharma was preached for the good of humanity at large. The devas, the four mahārājikas, and the gods of the Tāvatiṁsa, Yāma, and Tuṣita heaven began to praise the Buddha. This was the consequence of the Buddha's second dream. In the third dream he saw many red-coloured creatures with black heads covering him up to the knee. This dream was interpreted in this way that many people followed the religious path shown by him and went to heaven after death.

In the fourth dream he saw four birds of various colours came from the four directions through the sky and became white after touching his feet. It was interpreted thus. The Brāhmins, the Kṣatriyas, the Vaiśyas, and the Śūdras became liberated after having accepted his dharma. In the fifth dream he saw that he was roaming about on the Miḷa mountain of great height. The effect of this dream was that he was honoured everywhere and everybody embraced his doctrine.

The Bodhisattva thought that it was difficult to practise celibacy while leading a household life. He determined to renounce the world. He informed the king of his determination. Śuddhodana tried his utmost to induce him to give up his determination. He also told the prince that he would be cut up with grief and his mother would die if the prince would renounce the world. He then asked his son to practise dharma at home. He sent for five hundred kings who came and asked the prince not to renounce the world. The Bodhisattva told the kings that he would not leave the world if his father could stand as a surety against four things. The kings said this to King Śuddhodana who wanted to know the four things. The Bodhisattva prayed to his father (1) for everlasting youth so that old age might not seize him; (2) for perpetual freedom from disease; (3) for immortality so that death might not carry him away; and (4) for eternally living in riches so that misfortune might not afflict him. Gods heard of this and were greatly delighted. King Śuddhodana said to the prince with an aggrieved heart and tears in his eyes that it was not unknown to the prince that worldly creatures were not free from old age, disease, death, and distress. Then the prince assured the king that he would not leave the world if the king could stand as a surety against three things, *viz.*, my passion (kāmaguṇa) might be celestial, always pleasant and beneficial. The king said that in this world kāma (sensual pleasure) was not pleasant and beneficial. Then the prince asked the king to be a surety against two things, *viz.*, pride and appropriation from which he desired to be free for ever. The king said with tears in his eyes that he had never heard of this and he expressed his inability to be a surety. The prince then requested the king to guarantee at least one thing, *viz.*, that during his residence there in that great palace his unrestrained mind might remain under his control. King Śuddhodana, unable to comply with his request, began to shed tears. Bodhisattva said thus,—"There is no doubt that I shall be free from old age and death, from the fear of affliction and that I shall acquire perpetual happiness. Please drive away your grief and be patient".

Thereafter, the Bodhisattva began his meditation under the shadow of a Jambu tree. King Śuddhodana noticed this and thought that the words of the sage, Asita, would be fulfilled if the prince were devoted to peaceful meditation. He made up his mind to build a spacious harem with beautiful gardens where the prince would be immersed in sensual pleasures and would never think of renunciation. The king carried out his resolve. He brought a large number of women and built many pavilions which were decorated with flowers and gems. The king asked the women to engage the prince with dancing and music so that he might not think of renunciation. The prince did not find delight in dancing and music. He became disgusted with the world. His mind was greatly agitated. He did not find delight in beautiful women. The king entered the harem and enquired about the health of the prince as there was no music going on there. The king was informed by the goddess of the Lumbinivana from the heaven that the prince was not attached to the world, he would soon cut off the tie and repair to a forest where penances were practised. Even surrounded by women in the palace he was thinking of the impermanence of the body. The king became sad and went to the prince and enquired of him whether he was keeping well and why he was sitting there with a pale face, full of sorrow. The prince said, "I find disease in body; disease attacks recovery (ārogya), death attacks life. All saṁkhāras[1] (confections) are subject to decay. Life is decaying, season after season, year after year; death becomes imminent. This is the perturbed state of health. I also find the impermanence of wealth; wealth is something like illusion; it deceives people and brings about quarrel. There is no permanent stability of wealth". The king said, "Son! Don't think of this. You are now young. Engage yourself

---

[1] Saṁkhāra constitutes rūpa, vedanā, saññā, saṁkhāra, and viññāna.

in kingly duties, find delight in the spacious harem, do not think of renunciation". The prince replied, "Father, if you can grant me the eight boons, I shall never think of this". After the king had promised to grant the boons, the prince enumerated them thus, "Old age should not attack my youthful days; let not disease attack me who am now free from disease, let not death attack me who am now alive; never should there be a separation between yourself and myself; let not all our relatives share suffering in this world; let all persons be free from suffering, let me not be subject to birth, old age, and death". The king replied, "I have no such power, my ancestors, King Dṛḍadhanu, Niśāntāyu, Yugandhara, and others, too, had no such power". The king then told the prince to renounce the world after his (king's) death. But the prince said, "Father, you will find me perfectly enlightened, free from desire, suffering, and sorrow during your lifetime". The king failed to win the prince over to his side with the help of women who were dancers and musicians. Even the palace, like the abode of gods, could not please the prince. The prince took the world to be a stage. He said to his father thus, "If there were no old age, disease, or death in this world, if there had been eternal happiness in this world, if there had been no eternal fear in this world, then and then only he would have been attached to this world, otherwise not". The king could not change the mind of the prince in any way. He determined to bring all the girls of Kapilavastu before the prince to captivate his mind. The prince expressed his desire to see the girls. By the king's order the path leading to the garden was decorated, well-scented, and royal officers were stationed at different places and arrangements were made to prevent old, diseased, blind, and other disabled persons from coming in front of the prince. The prince started towards the garden in a carriage decorated with seven kinds of gems. The subjects welcomed him with folded hands and various kinds of scents and powders were showered upon him. The Suddhāvāsadevaputras and other deva-putras placed a worn-out person on the way. The Bodhisattva seeing this old man with grey hairs, bent down and walking with the help of a stick asked the charioteer thus, "Who is that person?" The charioteer replied, "That person is old and has acquired this state due to old age". The prince said to the charioteer, "We shall be subject to such old age. We cannot do away with it. If old age comes, then what is the use of enjoyment in the garden? Turn back the chariot, I shall not go to the garden". The prince returned and the king was informed of the cause of the prince's returning home. The king made especial arrangements for dancing and music in the palace. But the prince did not find delight in them. He began to think of that old person. On another day, the prince again wanted to go to the garden. The king arranged that there should be no horrible sight in the path leading to the garden. The Suddhāvāsadevaputras and other gods created in that path a diseased person whose hands and feet were thin, face pale, belly inflated, and water streaming down the belly. The Bodhisattva seeing him asked the charioteer, "What is this?" The charioteer replied, "This person is diseased. What is the good of knowing him. Let us go to the garden". The prince replied, "What is the use of staying in this world where there are old age and disease? I shall not go to the garden". He returned home and began to think of the old and diseased persons. The king tried his best by music and dancing to attract his mind but in vain. Again he wished to go to the garden. The devaputras this time created a dead person in the way. The dead body was being carried and placed on a bedstead. The relatives were carrying it and crying. Some were seen striking their breast, some were seen uprooting the hair of their heads, and others were lamenting. Seeing this sight the prince became moved. On enquiry, he learnt from his charioteer that the deceased could no more see his parents, brothers, and others, nor would he be able to see the Jambudīpa. The prince began to think thus, "Death is no friend of or enemy to anybody. As seasons change regularly so does death approach. All are equal in the eye of death. It levels equally the rich and the poor.

Where is happiness in this world where there are old age, disease, and death?" The prince did not proceed further but he returned home.

Once more he desired to go to the garden. This time he saw on the way a yellow-robed monk with senses controlled. The prince asked him about the cause of his renouncing worldly life. He (the monk) replied, "He has renounced the worldly life to control his own self and to attain parinirvāṇa". The prince became pleased with him. At this time, Ānanda's mother named Mṛgī, a Sākya girl, came to the prince and told him, "Your parents are happy (nirvṛta)[1] and the girl whose husband you would become is also happy (nirvṛta)". The prince heard the word "Nibbuta" and took it in the sense of nirvāṇa. He began to think of nirvāṇa only and could not see Mṛgī nor could he hear her word. King Śuddhodana built a big door named Ṣadvālaka for the palace. Five hundred persons were needed to open the door. The opening of the door produced a sound that travelled to a distance of a yojana. Five hundred kings surrounded the city so that the prince might not go out of the palace. King Śuddhodana began to make arrangements for anointing the prince on the day when the star named Puṣyā would predominate. The prince, too, thought of renouncing the world at the same time. Sons of the gods came to him and reminded him of renunciation. Unless he set out he would be a

---

1 *Nibbuto (in Pāli)*—one who is calmed. It means Nirvāṇa.

religious sovereign of the four islands. The four great islands, viz., Jambudvīpa, East Vedeha, Aparagodānika, and Uttarakuru would be under his rule.

Rāhula entered the womb of Yaśodharā in the middle watch of the night, having fallen from the Tuṣita heaven. The Bodhisattva awoke and saw all sleeping in the harem. Some were seen sleeping with lute on their lap, some embracing the musical instrument, some placing the musical instrument on the head, and some embracing one another. Some were sleeping with saliva coming out of their mouth. The harem appeared to him to be a cemetery. He rose up from his bedstead. He took a fine Kāśī Cādar (cover) and asked Chandaka to bring the horse, Kaṇṭhaka. Chandaka tried his best to induce the prince to reconsider the matter. The prince refused to take his advice. Chandaka brought Kaṇṭhaka shouting at the top of his voice with the object of causing the king to awake. But through the influence of the gods none awoke. Kaṇṭhaka, too, made a loud noise. The Bodhisattva rode on the horse Kaṇṭhaka and marched on. Showers of flowers poured forth from the sky and the heavenly nymphs began to sing songs. The Yakkha, named Supratiṣṭhita, with a retinue of five hundred, opened the door, named Ṣadvālaka, without any sound. The Bodhisattva renounced the world, while young and not old, keeping sound health and not suffering from ailment, in the enjoyment of riches and not in poverty, having many relations and not bereft of kinsmen. At the time of his departure from the palace all the mountains trembled, the ocean became agitated, and gods poured forth sandal-powders. The whole earth was lighted. Darkness was dispelled and all beings were filled with joy. Only the abode of Māra[1] remained gloomy and his heart appeared to have been struck with an arrow. The sun, the moon, the stars, and the heavenly abodes became purified. All people began to worship the Bodhisattva. Both gods and men welcomed him. The Bodhisattva came out of Kapilavastu and said, "I shall go to hell and take poison, yet I shall not return without overcoming old age and death".

The Bodhisattva was brought to Anomiya, a city near the hermitage of Vaśiṣṭha in the Malla-kingdom[2] to the south of Kapilavastu at a distance of twelve Yojanas. Here the Bodhisattva made over to Chandaka his garment, the horse Kaṇṭhaka, and the umbrella, and asked him to convey his good news to Mahāprajāpatī Gautamī, father Śuddhodana, and his relatives, and to inform them that he would come back to them after having been successful in establishing the best religion.

The Bodhisattva cut off his hair with his sword. The hair was brought by Indra and worshipped in the Tāvatiṁsa Heaven. Kaṇṭhaka began to lick his feet. The Bodhisattva did not wait but he went on. The Bodhisattva sent good news to all except

---

1 Māra is Buddhist Satan.

2 Vide my "Some Ksatriya Tribes of Ancient India"—Mallas.

Yaśodharā. The Blessed One was asked by the bhikkhus why he did not care for Yaśodharā. The Blessed One replied that not only in that life but also in previous births, he did not care for her. As requested by the Bhikkhus, the Buddha narrated the Śyāmā and the Campakanāgarāja Jātakas.

The Bodhisattva having renounced the world, Chandaka and Kaṇṭhaka returned to Kapilavastu from Anomiya. King Śuddhodana, Yaśodharā, and others wept in the palace. Chandaka related every thing to them. Kaṇṭhaka being cut up with grief, died and was reborn as the son of god Śikhaṇḍi and enjoyed celestial bliss. (Cf. Kaṇṭhaka Jātaka.)

The Śuddhāvāsa devaputras (gods dwelling in the Śuddhāvāsa heaven) created a yellow robed hunter in that forest. The Bodhisattva went to the hunter and gave to him his Kāśī cloth in exchange for his yellow robe. Then the Bodhisattva entered Vaśiṣṭha's dharmāraṇya and the hermitage of Vaśiṣṭha became illuminated. Vaśiṣṭha seeing him became astounded. The disciples of the sage gave him various fruits to eat. Questioned by Vaśiṣṭha, the Bodhisattva spoke out his identity and told him the object of his becoming a religious mendicant. Vaśiṣṭha blessed him. The Bodhisattva then went to Vaiśālī and accepted Ārāḍa Kālāma as his guru. He considered the dharma instructed by Kālāma to be unfavourable for the attainment of salvation. So he went to Rājagṛha where the king of Magadha saw him on his round for alms. The king was charmed by his handsome appearance and after enquiry came to know that the Bodhisattva was dwelling at the Pāṇḍava Hill. The king of Magadha with his officers approached the Bodhisattva, sat at his feet, and asked him who he was. The Bodhisattva spoke out his identity and told him the object of his renouncing worldly life. The king requested him thus, "After acquiring perfect knowledge, please come and give me instructions in the dhamma". The Bodhisattva promised to do so. Then Bodhisattva accepted Udraka, son of Rāma, as his guru, but he left him considering his instructions in the dhamma to be of little aid in obtaining nirvāṇa. He came to Gayā where at the Gayāśirṣa mountain three similies crossed his mind. He then went to the village of Uruvilvā from Gayāśirṣa. Puraṇa Kāśyapa, too, came to the same village for alms. The Bodhisattva went to the house of a village headman for alms. Sujātā, the daughter of the village headman, together with her husband stood in front of the Buddha with eyes full of tears. Sujātā offered the Buddha honeyed rice-gruel. The Buddha asked her the object of her offering. Sujātā said that Śuddhodana's son, Gautama, had renounced the world for six years. She had made this offering wishing the fulfilment of his mission. At this very moment a celestial voice said, "Sujātā! This is the same Gautama". With folded hands and trembling body, Sujātā said, "For six years I did not sleep thinking of your austerity. To-day my mind is satisfied". The Buddha said, "You were my mother in 500 previous births". The Bodhisattva went out of Uruvilvā with a pot full of cakes. But Puraṇa Kāśyapa's pot always remained empty. He was asked by the Bodhisattva as to how much alms he had received. Kāśyapa said that he had not received any alms in the sinful villages, namely, Praskandaka Vatakalpa, Ujjaṁgala, and Jaṁgala. The Bodhisattva, however, said that he had received plenty of alms in these gentle villages.

On Bodhisattva's renunciation of the world, King Śuddhodana daily used to get news about him whereever he happened to be. Once the Bodhisattva stopped inhalation and exhalation, the messenger thought that he had breathed his last. The king was informed accordingly, and he believed that the prince could not die as he was showing wonderful signs since his birth. The king thought that most probably he had become absorbed in meditation and the messengers had taken him to be dead. The king asked the messengers to enquire once again. They again came to Uruvilvā and were astounded to see the prince in good health.

The Bhikkhus asked the Buddha why King Śuddhodana did not believe that he (the prince) had died. The Buddha replied that formerly King Śuddhodana did not believe that (Cf. Śyāmaka Jātaka).

The Bodhisattva, while at Uruvilvā, practised severe austerities. For eighteen months he used to take one plum daily, for a further period of 18 months, he used to take one sesamum seed daily; for 18 months more he used to take one grain of rice every day and for 18 months he did not take anything. He became lean and thin. His body became so weak that death seemed to be imminent. Devas, asuras, and men became amazed to see his severe austerities. King Śuddhodana, Mahāprajāpatī Gautamī, Yaśodharā, and the Sākyans became very much anxious to hear of the severe austerities from messengers. Yaśodharā gave up food, put on ordinary clothes, and spent her days lying on bed of grass. When the Buddha was engaged in giving religious instructions at Rājagṛha, King Śuddhodana sent there Chandaka and Kālodāyī as messengers. They went there and requested the Buddha to be compassionate to his relatives. The Blessed one asked them to accept ordination. They assured him that they would comply with his request by the permission of the king. Then at the will of the Buddha, the householder's mark on them vanished and there appeared monks' robes and alms-bowls. Chandaka and Kālodāyī then accepted ordination.

Udāyī informed the Buddha about the severe vow of Yaśodharā. The Bhikkhus asked the Buddha why Yaśodharā was so much attached to him. The Buddha then related the Mṛgarāja Jātaka and intimated them that in previous births she was also attached to him.

The Bodhisattva was engaged in severe austerities near the bank of the Nairañjanā river in a forest at Uruvilvā. At that time Māra came and told him thus, "What is the good of renunciation? Be a householder, you will be a supreme ruler and by performing the Aśwamedha sacrifice and such other sacrifices you will accumulate much merit. Renunciation is very difficult". The Bodhisattva replied, "I don't want merit, I am not immortal, I am subject to death. I shall attain salvation by leading the life of a Brahmacārī. A river may be dried up by wind yet my blood cannot be dried up; let my body be dried up, my mind will still be pleased. Recollection, vivacity, and meditation must exist. If I attain the excellent path, I shall surely attain purity of Sattva (soul). My desire, strength, and wisdom have not decreased. If I do not attain the way to nirvāṇa at the foot of the Bodhi tree, Māra's army will not be destroyed. Victory is attained by the strong only. I shall destroy Māra's army by my wisdom. Boy or unwise person commits mistakes". Listening to the words of the Bodhisattva, Māra disappeared. For six years the Bodhisattva was engaged in severe austerity. During this period, Māra made several attempts to ruin the Bodhisattva but in vain. It is to be noted that in former births the Bodhisattva performed severe austerity to attain salvation. (Cf. Śakuntajātakakathā, the Kacchapa Jātaka, Markaṭa Jātaka, the Śakuntaka and the Surupamṛgarāja Jātakas).

Once upon a time, the Blessed one was roaming about with 500 monks in the Gṛdhrakūṭa mountain at Rājagṛha. Nanda, Sunanda, Sumana, Iśvara, Maheśvara and other Śuddhāvāsa gods beautified the Gṛdhrakūṭa mountain by their person just at the time night passed over and they came to the Blessed one, touched his feet with their heads and saluted him with folded hands. Devaputra Nanda told the Tathāgata thus, "The Perfectly Enlightened Tathāgatas of previous ages explained the Avalokita Sūtra. It would be beneficial to humanity at large if the bhikkhus could listen to your explanation". Devaputras saying thus disappeared and the Blessed one explained the Avalokita Sūtra to the Bhikkhus. While the Bodhisattva was beholding from one side of the river to the other, the Mahāśākya devas versed in previous religions worshipped him. Indra, Suddhāvāsa devas, and other gods acquired the pleasant religion. The Bodhisattvas were endowed with various kinds of strength in body, mind, and speech. They used to live in that world where they killed the powerful Yakṣa, defeated the great army, crossed the vast ocean, became the chief of men, obtained sincerity and perfect enlightenment and did what they said, said what they did, treated the five elements equally, won success and acquired proficiency in body, mind, and speech. That part of the world where the Bodhisattva killed the Yakkhas was divided into sixteen parts. After performing severe austerities in Uruvilvā, the Bodhisattva with rice-gruel offered by Sujātā, came to the banks of the river, Nairañjanā, took his bath, and partook of the rice-gruel. Leaving the white-copper (kaṁsa) pot he took rest for sometime and considered the conduct he had to lead. Thereafter, he started for the place where stood the Bodhi tree. On the way he begged grass from a grass-dealer named Svastika. When he reached the Bodhi tree he did not see Māra there. But Māra saw him. Five hundred peacocks, lotuses, curlews, cranes, pitchers full of water, and girls circumambulated the Bodhisattva who thought that this was the prognostication of the attainment of perfect enlightenment. Nāga king, named Kāla, told the Bodhisattva that he would surely obtain perfect enlightenment that day like Krakucchanda, Konākamuni, and Kāśyapa. The Bodhisattva then sat in meditation at the foot of the Bo-tree. Māra commenced to sing songs in front of the Bodhisattva but he was threatened by Bodhisattva by fourteen kinds of horrible sights. (Cf. Jyotiṣkagṛhapati Jātaka.)

Māra began to lament. Again he came to the foot of the Bodhi tree with his Caturaṅginī[1] army (fourfold army) and made a loud sound. The Bodhisattva acquired the first Jhāna. Gradually he acquired the second, the third, and the fourth Jhānas. Then he arrived at a stage which

[1] A complete army, consisting of four members, *viz.*, elephants, chariots, horses, and foot soldiers.

was beyond happiness and suffering and acquired purified recollection (Smṛtipariśuddha). In the first watch of the night, he gained celestial insight and by virtue thereof he discerned the people's course of life born of virtue and vice. In the middle watch of the night, he recollected thousands and thousands of his former births. In the last watch of the night, he attained supreme enlightenment by means of acute concentration. He realised suffering, origin of suffering, cessation of suffering, and the path leading to the cessation of suffering. He further realised that knowledge arises from ignorance, *i.e.*, when ignorance is dispelled, knowledge is originated, from knowledge come Nāmarūpa (Name and Form); thus six senses, contact, sensation, desire, old age, disease, and death come into being. Knowledge springs up on the destruction of ignorance and causes the disappearance of misery. This is Nirvāṇa. Then he thought that happiness was the reward of virtue. Māra could not stand in the way of a virtuous man. A virtuous man would acquire what he would desire to have and could attain Nirvāṇa. The Buddha said that by virtue of wisdom he was liberated from misery and that Māra with his army had been defeated and reduced to ashes.

Many millions of Devas worshipped the Buddha seated on one seat for a week. Celestial flowers were showered on him. The Śuddhāvāsa and Kāyika devas approached and worshipped him. Māra was threatened by eighty kinds of sights.

Once upon a time, the Buddha was dwelling in Āmrapāli's mango grove at Vaiśālī with a large number of Bhikkhus. At that time a Bhikkhu named Viśuddhamati saluted the Buddha and requested him to relate for the welfare and happiness of the world what he had seen as a Bodhisattva while on the miraculous throne under the Bodhi tree (Bodhimaṇḍo). The Buddha praised Viśuddhamati for putting to him this question and said the following in compliance with his request. When the Bodhisattva entered into the womb of the queen, in the guise of a nāga elephant from the Tuṣita heaven, all the world trembled. When the Bodhisattva was born, Indra himself held the cloth as bright as gold. Immediately after birth when the Bodhisattva advanced seven steps to destroy old age, disease, and death, the earth quaked, all sides were illuminated, divine sound was heard from heaven, divine powders and flowers were showered. The Bodhisattva gave up the kingdom at the age of 29 and put on yellow robe. After becoming a religious mendicant, he engaged himself in severe austerity for 12 years. Then he entered into the kingdom of Magadha. He met and received welcome from Sujātā, the daughter of a villager. Sujātā said that King Bimbisāra had a great gain that day. In his kingdom, Bodhisattva had acquired incomparable enlightenment.

The Bodhisattva reached the bank of the river Nairañjanā. The earth quaked, the ocean became agitated, the Yakkhas, the Gandharvas, the Asuras, the king of all birds, the Kinnaras, and others became delighted.

Then he crossed the river Nairañjanā. Eighty crores of gold umbrellas were held over the head of the Bodhisattva. The Nāga king, named Kāla, with his retinue came there and saluted him. For the achievement of the same end Bodhisattva came to the same spot, *viz.*, the foot of that very Bodhi tree where Krakucchanda, Konākamuni, and Kāśyapamuni came to attain perfect enlightenment. The assembly of gods gladly showered flowers on the Bodhisattva. The Suddhāvāsadevas decorated him with mandāra flowers and perfumed wind blew. The lustre of his person illuminated all sides. The nāga king, named Kāla, heard this incomparable sound and came there with his daughters, worshipped the Bodhisattva and said, "I notice in you the same marks as I found on the person of Krakucchanda, Konākamuni, and Kāśyapa. Gods have come here to worship you. To-day you will surely attain Buddhahood and the unique abstract contemplation of God (Samādhi)". On hearing the words of Kāla, Bodhisattva gladly came to the foot of the Bodhi tree. At this time the Bo-tree was variously decorated. Gods from heaven worshipped the Bodhisattva with flowers, incense, etc. The Bodhisattva thrice went round the Bodhi tree and sat on his own seat after recollecting the former Tathāgatas. His face became bright. He fully realised that he would not be able to attain perfect enlightenment unless he could defeat Māra. Māra came there with his fourfold army. He could not tolerate the austerity of Bodhisattva.

Māra's defeat by the Buddha

The Śākya prince who was Svayambhu (self-created one) and of sacred personality came to the foot of the Bodhi tree and brightened all sides. Māra became frightened. Gods decorated the Bo-tree with various kinds of gems. The Bodhisattva was firm and sat motionless. Māra put on a coat-of-mail and came there. His heart trembled. He began to praise the Bodhisattva thus, "You are incomparable in beauty, your colour is unique. Like the moon free from cloud you have overwhelmed the devas, nāgas, and men; you have seven gems; your body is endowed with thirty-two signs of a great man. Find delight in woman and be a supreme ruler. You will be blessed with thousands of powerful sons who will conquer the earth. Girls of Māra are singing songs for your delight, some are throwing scented powders. O, prince, stay in the palace and enjoy life". The Bodhisattva replied, "I shall be the lord of the world by attaining Buddhahood, I shall conquer earth by acquiring four miraculous powers. Kāma (lust) gives no pleasure rather it leads one to hell. I have no desire for kāma. It is abominable. I shall surely attain salvation. The Bodhisattva is not at all attached to women because they are the cause of various kinds of injury. To me don't speak highly of kāma". Māra's

(*Copyright, Archæological Survey of India*)

Māra tempting Buddha

son, Svārthavāha, said to his father thus, "Please excuse my impertinence and listen to me. The earth quaked during his birth. The ten quarters were illuminated. Divine instruments were played upon from heaven. Divine umbrellas were held by gods. Flags were hoisted. Bodhisattva will be the eye of all. He will dispel ignorance and will be the saviour of the world. He will do good to the world, will defeat the army of Māra. He will overpower Brahmā, Sakra, Guhyaka (a demi-god and attendant of the god of wealth), nāga, asura, Manuja, and mahoraga. He cannot be moved in any way from this Bodhi tree". Māra was sorry and told his son in reply, "O, boy, don't frighten me. I shall put obstacles in the way of the Bodhisattva with the help of my army. You are my eldest son and yet you are a follower of Gautama! Why are you paralysing the activity of my army?" Svārthavāha further told his father, "One cannot live in this world by doing injury to the Bodhisattva. Who will move the Bodhisattva? Your army will be frightened at his sight. Your army will be destroyed by him. At the foot of this Bodhi tree, Krakucchanda, Konāka, Kāśyapa, and 4,000 Buddhas attained saṁbodhi and this Bodhisattva will also acquire enlightenment". Svārthavāha then worshipped the Bodhisattva. Māra's army attacked the Bodhisattva but the latter remained firm. Māra's army got frightened and fled. Māra silently began to think. The Bodhisattva thought of suffering, origin of suffering, and cessation of suffering. The Devaputras worshipped him. Sitting on one seat he meditated for a week and after having acquired Bodhi he did not get up from his seat. The devas showered flowers from the sky for seven nights continually. Māra was defeated. The world felt happy. Fire became pacified and creatures gave up envy. The Bodhi tree was decorated with banners, umbrellas, etc. Diseased and aggrieved people became free from illness and grief. The man born blind got back eyesight. The Tathāgata was pure in precept, in meditation, in wisdom, in emancipation, in the knowledge of emancipation, love, and compassion. Eternal bliss is obtained by the worshipping of such a pure Tathāgata.

The Bodhisattva acquired five saññā (consciousness). Māra himself approached the Bodhisattva and saluted him. When Māra asked the Bodhisattva to stay in the palace and to enjoy kingly enjoyments, the latter asked him why he had come there and told him that his object had already been frustrated. Māra again came to the sky and the Bodhisattva again asked him who he was. When Māra introduced himself to him and threatened him that he would attack him with his army, the Bodhisattva said that even koṭis of Māras would not be able to do him any injury. Māra made several vain attempts to frustrate the object of the Bodhisattva. In the first watch of the night he fled. Gautama acquired divine vision. In the second watch he remembered previous births; and on sunrise, he acquired perfect enlightenment. Gautama said, "Profound divine meditation known as 'Lokavijita' is attainable. The world is full of suffering, where there is birth there is suffering, it is better to lead the life of a brahmacārī. Suffering originates from upadhi (attachment). Suffering is not engendered on the destruction of attachment. Creatures are ephemeral and are subject to suffering. On the destruction of the desire for existence (Bhavatṛṣṇā), fear disappears. Destruction of desire (tṛṣṇā) is Nirvāṇa. One who has attained Nirvāṇa is not born again. Māra gets overwhelmed; enemy is conquered; all sorts of fear are dispelled. A person who has obtained Nirvāṇa is not subject to rebirth. Māra is defeated by him. He is free from all fears" (cf. Kuśa Jātaka).

Gautama's principal disciples

Once the Buddha's disciple, Ānanda with five hundred bhikkhus, was staying at Veluvana in Rājagṛha in Magadha. Mahākāśyapa heard of the weakness, supineness, and laxity of thirty disciples of Ānanda and came there. After an exchange of friendly greetings Mahākāśyapa asked, 'why has the Lord Buddha prohibited eating in an assemblage (gana bhojana)? Why has he approved trikbhojana (dinner of three persons)?" Ānanda failed to reply. Mahākāśyapa himself answered, "The Buddha has done so for the preservation of the householders and for the destruction of sin. O,

Long lived Kumar Ānanda, you are not proving your knowledge in all things (mātrajñatā) by begging alms with your disciples". Ānanda was surprised at the use of the word 'Kumāra' and said, "My hairs have turned grey, yet you call me a Kumāra".

Mahākāśyapa thrice addressed him as Kumāra. The Bhikkhuṇī Sthulanandā heard of Mahākāśyapa calling Ānanda a Kumāra and said, "Reverend Mahākāśyapa! Why do you address Ānanda, the favourite disciple of the Buddha, as Kumāra"? Ānanda at once said, "Reverend Mahākāśyapa, please pardon these ignorant mothers". Then Mahākāśyapa said to Ānanda, "On receiving ordination I did not take counsel from any person other than the Buddha. When I was sick of household life; when I had a strong desire for celibacy, I renounced vast wealth and started in search of the Lord Arahat. I found the Lord in the Bahuputra Caitya at Rājagṛha, saluted him touching his feet, and became his disciple. The Lord himself gave me various instructions. Thus did Mahākāśyapa gladden and encourage the bhikkhus with religious discourses and then left his seat. Sthulanandā was not satisfied. So she went to hell.

The rich village of Nālandā was at a distance of half a yojana from Rājagṛha. There lived in that village a wealthy brahmin who had several sons named Dharma, Upadharma, Śatadharma, Tiṣya, and Upatiṣya by his wife called Śārī. His youngest son, Upatiṣya, used to study the veda in his preceptor's house. There was a wealthy and largely populated village named Kolita situated at a distance of half a yojana from Rājagṛha. In this village there lived a rich brahmin of the Maudgalyāyana gotra. He had a learned and intelligent son, named Kolita, who too, studied the veda with a preceptor with whom five hundred disciples read. Kolita and Upatiṣya finished their study while in the preceptor's house. They were fast friends. There was a festival known as Giriyagrasamāja in Rājagṛha. Thousands of people assembled in hundreds of gardens. Songs were sung, musical instruments were played, theatrical performances were held with great pomp. Kolita and Upatiṣya with horses, chariots, and servants came to Rājagṛha to see the festival. Sāriputta saw the huge crowd and the sense of transitoriness of the world crossed his mind. He thought that none of this crowd would survive after a hundred years. He noticed the teeth of the laughing crowd and everything worldly appeared to him to be made of bones. Owing to their past merits both Sāriputra and Maudgalyāyana felt a disgust for the world and mutually confiding each other of their desire to renounce the world, they accepted ordination.

At this time a mendicant, named Sañjayī Vairaṭiputra, lived in a paribrājakārāma in Rājagṛha. Sāriputra and Maudgalyāyana accepted ordination from this mendicant. The former learnt the duties of a mendicant in one week while the latter did so in two weeks, but they recognised the inanity of the courtship of the good discipline. They separated themselves from each other and went out in quest of dharma. They came to an understanding that he who would learn the dharma, first would teach the other. At this time the Lord Buddha was roaming with thirteen hundred bhikkhus in Veluvana. Bhikkhu Upasena went out on begging with plates and alms-bowl. Sāriputra met him, questioned him about his master and, at the first words of Upasena, light entered his mind.

Sāriputra came to Maudgalyāyana who, at his countenance only, guessed the good news. At the only enunciation of the formulæ, "Ye dharmā hetuprabhavā, *etc.*," both of them detached themselves from the false doctrines and were penetrated with the most favourable dispositions. Both Sāriputra and Maudgalyāyana came to Sañjayin and tried in vain to drag him to the Buddha. They came to the Buddha followed by the five hundred disciples of Sañjayin. The Buddha foreseeing the arrival of his two principal disciples, had had seats prepared. Sāriputra and Maudgalyāyana saw the Buddha, paid him homage, and were ordained along with their five hundred companions. In reply to a question from Sāriputra, Bhagavat explained to him the chain of causation (pratityasamutpāda). In seven days Maudgalyāyana acquired supernatural faculties.

Sāriputra, in a fortnight, received the complete science.

Conversion of Chandaka and Udāyi by Buddha

The Buddha was staying at Rājagṛha. The Śākyas of Kapilavastu requested their king Śuddhodana to bring the Buddha from Rājagṛha to Kapilavastu. Śuddhodana sent to the Buddha, Chandaka and Kālodāyī, who were Buddha's friends from childhood. Chandaka and Udāyi came to the Buddha and told him about their mission but within a short time both of them accepted ordination. The Lord preached the Dharma for seven years; then at the request of the Śākyas he expressed his desire to come to Kapilavastu. He started with the Bhikkhusaṃgha. When the Lord reached Kośala, the Śākyas set out in various cars to meet him. When the bhikkhus entered Kapilavastu from Nyagrodhārāma for alms, the king saw their bald heads and alms-bowl, and in disgust stopped them from going further.

Śuddhodana and the Buddha

The Lord did not give his consent when Uruvilvā Kāśyapa, Nadīkāśyapa, Gayākāśyapa, and Upasena wanted to see king Śuddhodana to pacify him. Mahāmaudgalyāyana sent Kālodāyī to pacify Śuddhodana. Kālodāyī made an aerial journey from Nyagrodhārāma and reached Kapilavastu. He stayed in air in front of the king. The king heard of the greatness of the Buddha and was highly satisfied. He started with his country men to see The Enlightened One. The king and the royal family went on in a chariot as far as the road permitted the chariot to be driven, then they walked on. On reaching Nyagrodhārāma, he made respectful obeisance to the aerial Buddha. The Lord showed various miracles while staying in the air. When he took his seat, Mahāprajāpatī Gotamī, Yaśodharā, and all other royal personages bowed down to the Lord's feet and sat on one side. The king put to the Buddha various questions and was much pleased to receive his answers.

Conversion of the Śākyas by the Buddha

The Buddha was then invited by his father, King Śuddhodana, who had the way from Kapilavastu to Nyagrodhārāma well decorated. When the Buddha and his disciples took their seats, they were treated to various edibles by the king. The Buddha, too, encouraged the king and his people with religious discourses. Thus one day Mahāprajāpatī, the second day, Yaśodharā, the third day, the women of the harem, then all the circle of the Śākyas received him with great hospitality. One day Yaśodharā invited the Buddha with his disciples and making over to Rāhula a cake which she had prepared, she told him to place it on the plate of the Buddha. Rāhula obeyed his mother and took his seat in such a place where the shadow of the Buddha fell on his body. Rāhula said to his mother that the shadow of the śramaṇas was very pleasant. Yaśodharā asked his son to pray for paternal property. Rāhula did so. The Buddha asked him to take holy orders and assured him that he would give him ancestral property. The king and the Śākyas were quite happy to hear of the assurance. Yaśodharā with all her attire and ornaments on served the Lord with food to induce him to come into the world but in vain. After taking his meal the Lord pleased and encouraged every body with various religious discourses and then went to Nyagrodhārāma.

King Śuddhodana consulted the Śākyas and ordered that a boy from every kṣatriya household should take holy orders and follow the Buddha. But the only son of a family need not take holy orders. Śuddhodana had two sons, Buddhadeva and Sundarananda. Buddhadeva took holy orders, Sundarananda did not do so. Out of three sons of Śuklodana, Devadatta renounced the world; Ānanda desired to renounce the world but he did not receive his brother's permission. He went to Videha and took the vow of silence. Nandan and Nandika, sons of Śukrodana, took holy orders. The other two sons stayed at home. Aniruddha, son of Amritodana, took holy orders. Thus five hundred Śākya lads took holy orders with splendour. All of them used various conveyances, such as elephant, horses, and carriages as far as roads permitted, then they walked on foot and reached Nyagrodhārāma. They saluted the Lord and took their seats.

Conversion of the Asuras by the Buddha

While at Nyagrodhārāma the Lord converted many persons to the faith by his three miracles, the miracle of the supernatural power, the miracle of instruction, and the miracle of the precept of the law. Sixty nayutas of asuras who came to pay homage to the Buddha, were converted and in accordance with their desire (pranidhi) obtained the promise to become one day as many Buddhas. At that moment the Exalted One smiled and with this smile sprang out rays of all shades that illuminated the whole Buddhakṣetra.

The venerable Aśvakin requested the Buddha to explain to him the reason of his smile. The Buddha said that he had smiled to hear of the desire of the asuras to attain Bodhi.

We like to record here a few more incidents of conversion into Buddhism by Gautama, the Buddha.

Bhagavat (Blessed one) arrived on the banks of the Ganges, after leaving the Ṛṣipatana, he recited some stanzas to the boatman who helped him across the great river. Bhagavat converted and ordained the boatman. On the boatman's asking the Buddha as to what he should reply when the people would ask him what he was, the Buddha told him to declare that he (the boatman) was a śramaṇa, a brāhmaṇa versed in the vedas, and an expert pilot.

Śakra took the appearance of a young man and followed the Buddha with all the necessaries

(Copyright, Archæological Survey of India)

Buddha's parinirvāṇa

of a hermit. When the people enquired about Śakra, the follower of the Buddha, Śakra said that he was the servant of Sugata. The Buddha sent him away.

PART II

STORIES

Mālinī

A Pratyeka-Buddha[1] entered into Kāśī for piṇḍas (alms) but receiving no alms, was walking out of the village. At this time, a villager was returning home after daily work. The villager said to the Pratyeka-Buddha, "Ārya, Have you received alms"? The Pratyeka-Buddha did not reply but he showed him the empty bowl. On seeing the empty bowl, the villager began to speak ill of other villagers and asked him to follow him for food. He entered the village with the Pratyeka-Buddha and coming to the cross-way he began to shout, "Utter ruin! Utter ruin!" On hearing this loud shout, villagers, males and females, assembled there and asked him what the matter was and why he was shouting so loudly. The villager said, "I am grieved to see the Pratyeka-Buddha going with empty hands". Then all the inhabitants of the village determined to treat the Pratyeka-Buddha with due hospitality. The villager invited the Pratyeka-Buddha with a view to honour him with food and raiment for life. He had a daughter

---

1 In Pali it is known as Paccekabuddha or individual Buddha. He is inferior to the sammāsambuddha. He is not omniscient. He has acquired the knowledge necessary to Nirvāṇa but does not preach it to men.

who was also informed of this arrangement. The daughter was highly pleased. The villager got a stūpa built in his honour in course of time. The daughter of the villager used to worship daily the stūpa with scents, garlands, incense, etc. This daughter was born in heaven. Hundreds of thousands of nymphs surrounded her and ornamented her head with various jewels. Descending from heaven, she was born in the womb of the queen of King Kṛki at Benares. She was named Mālinī.

The beautiful daughter of the king of Kāśī was of pure conduct and putting on pure garment, she used to stand before her father with folded hands. Her father entrusted to her the task of feeding the brahmins. Mālinī fed twenty-thousand brahmins, but on finding them desirous of her, she hated them and thought that they were not worthy of presents. She then found out the disciples of the Buddha and sent her maid to bring them to the palace. Mālinī, after causing them to sit on good seats, requested them to accept food. The disciples of the Buddha said that they would not accept anything unless something be given to them as the food for the Buddha. Mālinī replied that after taking food they should take with them some food for the Buddha and convey her desire to the Buddha to accept her invitation to the palace. The disciples after taking their meals brought some food for the Buddha and expressed to him her desire. The Buddha Kāśyapa accepted her invitation and having received this news she made arrangements for the food of the Buddha throughout the night. Next morning the Buddha Kāśyapa with his disciples including Tiṣya Bhāradvāja and others entered Benares. Buddha with twenty thousand disciples entered the inner apartments of King Kṛki. Mālinī welcomed the Buddha with his disciples and satisfied them with excellent food and drink. The Buddha Kāśyapa after washing his mouth gave religious instruction to her. The Brahmins grew angry with Mālinī because she fed the Buddha Kāśyapa with his disciples. At this time the influence of the brahmins was great. The brahmins resolved to kill her because she hated them and honoured the śramaṇas and was depriving the brahmins of the means of their livelihood.

The Brahmins sent a messenger to king Kṛki with the complaint that Mālinī was not showing reverence to the brahmins, and that, having brought Kāśyapa with his disciples to Rājagṛha, she had greatly honoured and worshipped him, while the brahmins were not given the opportunity to see her. She was not carrying out the instructions of the king. She was asked to feed twenty-thousand brahmins at Rājagṛha but in vain. The king came to Benares, and saw many brahmins assembled there. The brahmins offered their blessings to him and brought to his notice their grievances concerning Mālinī. They added, "If Mālinī lives then the brahmins will not daily obtain the thing which they usually get from your palace. If you want the state of a brahmin, you should renounce Mālinī." The king after considering much, thought it better to leave her. The king then sent a messenger to bring her inside the city. The messenger went to Rājagṛha and informed Mālinī thus, "The king has renounced you and the brahmins will kill you". Mālinī cried aloud in the presence of her mother and there was a great lamentation in the harem. All the inhabitants of the city became very much aggrieved to hear the news. Mālinī was brought before the king and she with folded hands requested the brahmins to allow her to say a few words, " O brahmins, I am now under your control and you have made up your mind to kill me. I pray for a week's time so that I can offer charity according to my desire and accumulate merit. After the lapse of the week you may either kill me or do whatever you like." The brahmins after much deliberation gave her time for a week. Then Mālinī informed her father that she would accumulate merit by offering charity for a week from to-day. Mālinī said, " I shall request Buddha Kāśyapa with his disciples to stay in the palace and accept my offerings." With the king's permission, Mālinī invited Kāśyapa to accept it. At this, the brahmins became angry and was anxious to kill her in course of the week. But Mālinī somehow pacified them. In the first day, Mālinī fed Kāśyapa with his disciples in the presence of her parents. Kāśyapa gave religious instructions to the king who gradually became a devotee with the female members of his harem. On the second day, five hundred sons became his followers. On the third day, the members of the family, on the fourth day, the royal officers, on the fifth day, the army, on the sixth day, the royal ācāryas (preceptors), and on the seventh day, all others became the followers of Kāśyapa. The king being pleased again invited Kāśyapa with his disciples. When all of them became attached to the religion of Kāśyapa, it struck them that it was owing to the influence of Mālinī that they acquired pure insight into all religions. They made up their mind to save Mālinī from the hands of the brahmins and they informed the brahmins that they must not kill her. All were assembled in the royal city and came before the brahmins. The brahmins seeing their strength informed the king that they would not kill Mālinī but they would try to subdue Kāśyapa who was responsible for all this. They sent ten persons well armed to kill Kāśyapa but as soon as they reached Kāśyapa, they became attached to the religion of the Buddha through the influence of his compassion. The Brahmins again sent twelve persons and they also became the followers of Kāśyapa. Afterwards thirty, forty, and fifty persons were sent successively to perform the same task but all of them became well-established in the Dharma of the Buddha and they afterwards sent a messenger to the remaining brahmins that Kāśyapa was a perfectly Enlightened One, compassionate and was always after the good of the world and they should not think of doing any injury to him. The remaining brahmins were further informed that they should come being free from haughtiness and pride to worship Kāśyapa. As soon as they received news they ran towards Kāśyapa with sticks in their hands but they were afterwards defeated by him.

Mañjarī Jātaka

In the past, there lived in Benares a brahmin belonging to the Kauśika gotra. Seeing the world full of miseries, he left the household life, became a monk, and built a hermitage near the Ganges. He acquired the four kinds of meditation and five kinds of Abhiññā (supernatural faculties). He became a great sage. He used to take food without giving it to any other person. One of his relatives was re-born after death by virtue of pious deeds as a gandharvaputra, named Pañcaśikha. In order to change his habit of taking food without giving it to any other person Pañcaśikha came to the hermitage with the sun, the moon, Mātali, and Indra, in the guise of brahmins, just at the time Kauśika was taking his food and asked for a share of his meal. At first, Kauśika was reluctant to part with a share of his meal; but on learning from them the merit of gift and their ancestry, Kauśika promised that he would not thenceforth partake of food, even nectar, without giving a share of it to śramaṇas and brāhmaṇas.

At this time, the four daughters of Indra, viz., Śrī (Goddess of prosperity), Śraddhā (Faith), Āśā (Hope), Hrī (Modesty) were worshipped with flowers by a sage. A dispute arose amongst them regarding individual's share of the flowers offered by the sage. In order to settle the dispute, the sage advised them to go to Indra and to seek his opinion as to who amongst them was the most superior. The daughters acted accordingly. Indra told them that they were all equal. The daughters were not satisfied at this. At their importunity Indra asked them to go to Kauśika, meanwhile, he sent nectar to Kauśika through Mātali. Kauśika would not drink it without giving a share of it to some other person. The daughters of Indra, Śrī, Śraddhā, Āśā, and Hrī prayed for nectar. Kauśika neglected the first three and gave nectar to Hrī. Indra again sent Mātali to Kauśika who came there and asked him the cause of indifference towards the first three. Kauśika said, "Śrī (Goddess of prosperity) goes lonely, Śraddhā (Faith) is evanescent, Āśā (Hope) is fruitless". Considering Hrī (Modesty) to be pure Kauśika gave nectar to her only. With this nectar, Hrī came to Indra and received the flowers offered by the sage. After death, Kauśika went to heaven. Kauśika was the Buddha and Hrī was Yaśodharā.

Godhā Jātaka

In ancient times, there reigned in Benares a king, named Suprabha. His son was named Suteja, who was loved by everybody. The king thought that as the prince was dear to one and all, his subjects might kill him (the king) and install his son on the throne. This thought led him to banish the prince. The latter with his wife lived in a hut near the Himalayas. He lived on fruits, vegetables, and the flesh of boars and deer. One day, while he went out of his hut, a cat killed an iguana, and kept it near the princess who did not touch it. Meanwhile, having collected fruits and vegetables, the prince returned and seeing the iguana the prince said to his wife, "whence has this iguana come?" The wife replied, "A cat has brought it here". The prince then peeled off the skin of the iguana and boiled it. His wife went to bring water. The prince thought that his wife did not even touch the iguana although she had a desire for eating its flesh. Had she had a little love for me, she would have cooked it. The prince, therefore, did not see any necessity of keeping some meat for his wife but he himself ate up the whole of the cooked iguana before his wife's return. On her return, the princess did not find the iguana but she learnt from her husband that the animal had fled. The princess was astonished at this impossibility and took it to heart that the prince had no love for her. In course of time, king Suprabha died and the ministers took the prince from the forest and made him king. On ascending the throne, the prince tried in vain to please his wife who had not then forgotten the iguana affair. The prince asked her about the cause of her dissatisfaction and learnt the true facts[1].

Hārapradāna Jātaka

At the time of the distribution of ornaments, Yaśodharā came last. The prince fixed his look on her. The prince took out from his own neck the most valuable necklace and gave it to Yaśodharā. The latter said, "Am I worthy to receive so much?" The prince forthwith took out of his finger the most valuable ring and gave it to her. Distributing all ornaments the prince entered the harem. The king learnt from his ministers that Yaśodharā, the daughter of Mahānāma, had attracted the prince's attention. The king prayed to Mahānāma for Yaśodharā. Mahānāma said, "The prince has been brought up in the harem. He has not learnt art, archery, politics, etc. He cannot be given a girl." The king was sorry. The prince heard of the cause of his father's sorrow and declared that on the seventh day from the day of declaration let all versed in art, archery, etc., come for competition. The king was delighted. Many persons came to the appointed place from Kapilavastu and various janapadas and Adhiṣṭhānas to see the prince's skill in art, archery, etc. At the door of the appointed place there was a powerful elephant. Prince Devadatta killed the elephant by one slap and being unable

---

[1] In Pali, there are two Godhā Jātakas, but the stories are different from what is stated above.

to move the huge animal, he walked over it. Prince Sundarananda saw the elephant on his way. He moved the elephant to a distance of seven feet from the door; still the door was blocked. Prince Sarbārthasiddha got down from the chariot and threw away the elephant beyond the seven walls (Prakāra) of Kapilavastu. People were astonished to notice the prince's prowess. The path was cleared. Every body went that way easily. Mahānāma too went that way.

Prince Sarbārthasiddha showed various feats. None could equal him in battle or boxing. At last arrows were shot. Seven palm trees were planted within twenty miles, each at a distance of two miles from the other. Some one's arrow went to the first palm tree, others to the second palm tree. Devadatta's arrow touched the third palm tree, Sundarananda's arrow passed the third palm tree, and dropped down between the third and the fourth palm trees. Bodhisattva got the arrow of his grandfather Simhahanu and said, "who can fix the arrow on this bow?" The assembly could not. The Śākya boys were asked to do it but they failed. Then, one after another, the Koliyas, the Licchavis were asked, they too failed. The Bodhisattva himself fixed the arrow on the bow of his grandfather after worshipping it with scents and garlands. Kapilavastu reverberated with the sound of the bow. The arrow passed the seven palm trees, pierced the earth and reached hell. Flower-rain was showered from the sky. Every one was pleased with the prince for his strength and prowess.

When the Bodhisattva came out and turned the wheel of Dharma, the bhikkhus heard of this and asked the Buddha about it. The Buddha replied that it was not in that birth but in previous births as well that he knew the Śākyas to have lost for ever the strength of their fist.

Vyagrībhūta Yaśodharā Jātaka

Once, at the foot of the Himalayas, all the quadrupeds assembled to select one of themselves to be their king. It was decided that he who would be able to reach the Himalaya mountain first would be selected king. A tigress reached the destination first. All the animals found that they were defeated by a female. Every where the king was male and no female ever reigned. The animals decided that one who would be married by the tigress would be the king of the quadrupeds. Ox, elephant, and lion wanted the tigress. The tigress forsook the first two and chose the lion as her husband. The Buddha was the lion at that birth and Yaśodharā, the tigress.

Dharmapāla Jātaka

In ancient times, there lived in Benares a king, named Brahmadatta. He had a learned priest named Brahmāyu. The latter sent his son, Dharmapāla, to a guru (preceptor) near the Himalayas, to learn the Vedas, etc. Near the hermitage of the preceptor, there was a lake where lived a monster (rākṣasa) who used to devour any person coming there to take a bath. Dharmapāla used to bathe in that lake where a nāga, a friend of Dharmapāla, used to live. His preceptor warned him against bathing in the lake. One day a boy resembling Dharmapāla went there to bathe. The monster ate him up partially. The half-eaten body floated on the surface of water. The brahmin pupils at once informed their teacher. The latter came to the spot, saw the half-eaten body which he thought to be that of Dharmapāla. He took it up. With bone and ash he came to Brahmāyu who said that such a thing could never happen. No body in his family had died young. Virtue alone saved the virtuous. Dharmapāla did not die. The Brahman came back to his house and was astonished to see Dharmapāla. In previous births, Buddha was Brahmāyu and his son Rāhula was Dharmapāla.

Śarakṣepaṇa Jātaka

In former ages, there lived in Benares a king whose kingdom extended up to Takṣaśīlā. The king installed his younger brother on the throne of Benares and went to live in Takṣaśīlā. At this time another king besieged Benares. The younger brother informed the king at Takṣaśīlā. The king wrote down something on a Bhurja leaf and wrapping the leaf round an arrow and binding it with a thread, he shot the arrow towards Benares. The arrow fell on the feet of the besieging king and broke into pieces the shield of his legs (pādaphalaka). The king thought that the arrow had been shot from Benares. He was greatly astonished. He took out from the arrow the Bhurjapatra and opening it found the following lines written therein:—"I break into pieces the shield of your leg. If you do not desire death, you should leave my kingdom." The king was afraid and astonished. He had a temple built there, established the arrow in it, and worshipped it. Thereafter he left Benares.

In that birth, Buddha was the king of Benares who shot the arrow from Takṣaśilā.

Amarā Jātaka

In days of yore, there was a village named Yavakacchaka situated at a distance of half a yojana from Mithilā. Outside Yavakacchaka there was a village of blacksmiths.

A blacksmith of that village had a learned daughter, named Amarā. A man of the Yavakacchaka village had a son, named Mahauṣadha. Once Mahauṣadha saw Amarā with rice on his way to the field. Mahauṣadha asked her who she was, what her name was, and so on. Amarā answered him in a riddle. Mahauṣadha understood her clearly. Both of them were attached to each other. Mahauṣadha went to Amarā's father and prayed for Amarā's hand. Amarā's parents told him that they would not marry their daughter to any body excepting a blacksmith. Mahauṣadha was intelligent and experienced in all the arts. He thought that the minutest work of the blacksmith was the manufacture of the needle. One able to manufacture the needle can do all sorts of blacksmith's works. He manufactured a wonderful needle and went to the village-smith to sell it. Amarā heard his voice and ran out to him and told him why he had come to sell needle in a place where such needles were manufactured. Mahauṣadha said, "Blacksmith will understand my skill in manufacturing needles so I have come here. If your parents know that I am skilled in preparing needles, they may give you to me."

Amarā told her father that this smith's son had manufactured a beautiful needle. Amarā's father marked his skill and gave him his daughter.

In this birth Buddha was Mahauṣadha, Yaśodharā was Amarā, and Mahānāma Śākya was the lord of the village-smiths.

Śiri Jātaka

In the past, there lived in the city Vāravāli, a brahmin well-versed in the three Vedas together with their glossaries and history. He had five hundred pupils whom he taught Vedamantras. He had a daughter of unique beauty, named Śiri. Once he was invited by a sacrificer, named Sārthavāha, living in a sea-port to perform sacrifice and was offered riches even if he would fail to attend personally. The brahmin called his pupils and said, "whoever will brave the journey to the sea-port will be given my daughter, Śiri". One of his pupils who was courageous and powerful and was already in deep love with Śiri wanted to go. He was sent by the brahmin with a letter to Sārthavāha. On reaching his destination, he made over the letter to Sārthavāha who read the letter and gave him gold and riches. The pupil bundled the riches and left the place. On his way home, the bundle fell into the sea during transhipment from the ship to the boat. He was sorely grieved and began to bale out the water of the sea. The sea-god appeared to him in the guise of a brahmin and asked him why he was making vain efforts. The boy said that he would worship the sea-god so long as he would not return him his riches. The sea-god was pleased and returned him his riches. He then won the hand of Śiri in exchange for gold and riches.

The Buddha identified the personages of the story by saying that in previous birth he was the disciple and Yaśodharā was Śiri. He won his wife after a strenuous endeavour.

Kinnarī Jātaka

In former ages, there reigned in Hastināpura a king, named Suvāhu, who had a handsome and meritorious son, named Sudhanu. Suvāhu entrusted the cares of the government to Sudhanu, the crown prince, and himself retired from royal affairs.

In the neighbouring town, known as Sinhapura, there reigned a king, named Sucandrima who was the friend of Suvāhu. Once king Sucandrima inaugurated a great sacrifice. He ordered hunters and fowlers to collect all animals, aquatic or moving on land. They did so. King Sucandrima invited those ṛṣis (sages) who had acquired four stages of mystic meditation, possessed five supernatural faculties (Pañca abhijñā) and great miraculous power and who could move about in the air. The sages came and said that all sorts of animals had been collected with the exception of the kinnarīs (fabled beings of the Himalayan region). As desired by the sages, the king sent the chief of the hunters to bring a Kinnarī. The hunter reached the hermitage of a sage in the Himalayas. The sage entertained him with fruits and water. At that time, the hunter heard sweet songs and learnt from the sage that Manoharā, the daughter of Druma, King of the Kinnaras, living in the Himalayas, used to come to the lotus-lake to sport with her female attendants, and that the Kinnara daughter and her attendants were then singing.

The hunter skilfully came to know from the sage that the Kinnarīs were brought under control by truthful words. The hunter came to the lotus lake. The kinnarīs were intoxicated with music and could not see him. Then the hunter said, "you are the daughter of Druma, king of Kinnaras and your name is Manoharā. You are bound by this truth. Manoharā! Don't walk a step further."

Manoharā was bound by the words of the hunter and was brought to Sinhapura. King Sucandrima rewarded the hunter and invited Suvāhu, King of Hastināpura, to attend the sacrifice. Suvāhu's son, Sudhanu, came to Sinhapura to honour the invitation but he was charmed with the beauty of the Kinnarī who, too, became attached to him. On enquiry, Sudhanu learnt from Sucandrima that the animals were brought for slaughter and that they would go to heaven being slain in the sacrifice. He further learnt that the sacrificer would go to heaven as many times as the number of animals he would slay in the sacrifice. Sudhanu said, "This is not true. Harmlessness is the best religion. Killing animals is a sin. To refrain from killing animals is religion."

Thus instructing on the tenfold virtuous paths of action, he said, "Man goes to heaven through these tenfold paths of action. Without these paths, he too goes hell."

King Sucandrima heard the words of Prince Sudhanu and let loose all the animals. Manoharā went with Sudhanu to Hastināpura. Sudhanu was so greatly attached to the Kinnarī that he neglected the royal duties. The ministers informed king Suvāhu of this. Suvāhu ordered the confinement of Sudhanu and the expulsion of the Kinnarī from the kingdom. The Kinnarī walked towards the Himalayas. Sometimes she turned her back to see whether Sudhanu was coming. When she reached the Satadru river, she gave a ring and garland to two fowlers, named Utpalaka and Mālaka, and told them to inform Sudhanu of her if Sudhanu happened to come that way. Then she crossed the river and proceeded to Mount Kailas. On the Kinnarī's departure, King Suvāhu released his son and had the harem decorated with various objects of luxury. This could not satisfy Sudhanu. He went out with his attendant, named Kaulaka, in search of the Kinnarī. On their way they met Utpalaka and Mālaka and came to know every thing. Utpalaka and Mālaka accompanied them. They reached the hermitage of the sage Kāśyapa, and gave him the description of the Kinnarī. The sage said that he had seen her go that way, and warned the prince against the dangers of the impassable way. When the prince did not stop, the sage requested the chief of the monkeys to accompany Sudhanu to the kingdom of the Kinnara King Druma. The chief of the monkeys took them on his back and reached the kingdom of the Kinnara rāj. On that day there was a grand festival in the city. On an enquiry Sudhanu learnt that the festival was in honour of the advent of Manoharā. He then threw his ring into the pot of one of those who came to bring water for Manoharā's bath without their knowledge. During the sprinkling of water that ring fell on Manoharā's lap. Manoharā saw the ring and understood that Sudhanu had come. She said this to her father, Druma, who received Sudhanu with great honour. Sudhanu stayed there with Manoharā for a long time. Then he received Druma's permission to go to Hastināpura with his family. King Druma was pleased and ordered the Yakṣa, named Yantaka, to accompany his daughter and son-in-law to Hastināpura. By the power of the Yakṣa, Sudhanu saw that he had come to the outer garden of Hastināpura the following morning. The gardener informed the king of his arrival. King Suvāhu had sought for his son in vain, and being sure of Sudhanu's death, he had performed his sradh ceremony.

Now he was delighted to hear of his son's arrival, rewarded the gardener, and received his son and daughter-in-law with great honour.

In his previous birth, Buddha was Sudhanu, Yaśodharā was Manoharā. Śuddhodana was Suvāhu and Mahānāma was Druma, Chandaka was Yantaka, Kanṭaka was the monkey-king. Rāhula was Utpalaka, Ānanda Thera was Mālaka, and Mahākāśyapa Thera was sage Kāśyapa of the Himalayas.

Story of Kuśa

King Ikṣvāku of Benares was childless. He used to allow the women of the harem to be known in the town on the 8th, 14th, and 15th day of every fortnight, in accordance with the suggestion of his purohita (the royal priest). Śakra did not approve of this conduct of the king. In the guise of an old brāhmaṇa, he came to the king who granted him the permission to choose a wife in the harem. He selected Alindā, the first queen, and took her away in spite of the reluctances of the queen and the hesitations of Ikṣvāku. During the night, Śakra revealed himself under his real appearance to Alindā and granted her a boon. The queen asked for a son and Śakra gave her a drug with direction to take it on the tip of her tongue, and declared that in punishment of her reluctances, her son, strong and wise, would be of an extreme ugliness. Śakra then disappeared. The queen came back to the King and related the adventure. The King got irritated at the prophesied ugliness and hid the drug; but the queen got a little of it from the stone where it had been ground for distribution to the other queens. Each one among the five hundred women gave birth to a son.

Kuśa, the son of queen Alindā, succeeded Ikṣvāku after his death. He claimed from his mother a beautiful queen. Sudarśanā, the daughter of the king of the Madrakas, was brought to him. But the couple met only in the dark. The princess complained of this sort of meeting to the queen-mother. Alindā replied to the protestations of the princess saying that they ought to see each other when Kuśa would be twelve years old. However, to appease her impatience Alindā permitted her daughter-in-law to see in a party given by the Court a pretended Kuśa, who was no one else but his brother Kuśadruma clad with the ensigns of royalty, while Kuśa played the part of the royal standard-bearer. Sudarśanā was delighted to see the king but no sooner did she notice the ugliness of the standard-bearer than she was struck with horror. She demanded the removal of this ugly person. But the pretended king, in praise of the standard-bearer, said to Sudarśanā that the standard-bearer being powerful, wealthy, heroic, and virtuous was his beloved associate.

Once on her return from the pond of lotus, Sudarśanā was asked by the king why she had not brought a lotus for him; but Sudarśanā said that while she had gone to the lotus-pond for bathing, she had fainted away to see a rākṣasa (demon) of the waters who resembled the standard-bearer. On another occasion after her return from the Mango-garden Sudarśanā was enquired by the King why she had not brought a mango for him; but she said that she had fainted away to see a rākṣasa (demon) of the wood who resembled the standard-bearer.

Once fire broke out in the elephant-stable, Kuśa girding up his loins, entered the stable, cut the chords with his sword, released the elephants, and himself extinguished the great fire. The harem praised him for his dexterity and vigour. Then Queen Sudarśanā found out, in despair, how her husband was ugly. She ran away to her father's house.

Kuśa installed his brother, Kuśadruma, on the throne and himself chased the fugitive towards the north with a Vīṇā (a seven-stringed musical instrument) in his hand. On his way, he passed the night in the house of an old woman who took him to be a demon from his eating up all that was offered him. Then he arrived at Kānyakubja.

On his entering the harem, he became a laughing stock of the women, and failed to conciliate Sudarśanā who disgracefully repulsed his advances and threats.

King Mahendraka reproached his daughter for having forsaken a powerful husband. He threatened to cut her into seven pieces and to give a piece of her to each of the besiegers of his town. Sudarśanā got frightened and went back to Kuśa. Sudarśanā's mother on seeing Kuśa in the harem could not recognise him to be her son-in-law and she questioned him about his parentage but the real name and power of Kuśa was revealed to her by her daughter. King Mahendraka heard of the presence of Kuśa in the harem and was sorry for not having been informed of this. Immediately the King greeted him with rich dishes and garments worthy of a king and Kuśa, too, allowed himself to be easily moved. As ordered by Kuśa, the ears of every man and animal of the town were closed and Kuśa uttered the shout of war like the roars of a lion. All the besiegers were assembled and each of them was given a daughter in marriage by the King and sent away. Then Kuśa left Kānyakubja with his wife. On his way, while looking at his shadow in the water, he was horrified by his own ugliness and was about to kill himself when Śakra gave him a jyotirasa stone which, while being worn on his head, would change him into the nicest man among all and while being covered with the hand, would give him again his first appearance. Kuśa wore the stone on his head and was transformed into the most handsome man. He returned to his capital.

At the end of the story, the bhikkhus asked the Exalted One why Kuśa was so ugly. The Lord said that his ugliness was due to his having, in a former existence, conceived unjust sentiments of envy when he found his young wife with a pratyekabuddha to whom she had just made an offering. Kuśa was at that time a man of the city of Kampilla. (Cf. Kusa Jātaka, Jātaka Edited by Faüsboll Vol. V.)

Story of Vṛṣabha

On being questioned by the Bhikkhus, Buddha said that it was not the only time that Māra had spied on him with a view to catch him, but in vain. He narrated the story of the jackal Girika who pursued the bull from which he hoped the testicles would come off and become his prey but was deceived by another jackal.

Story of Vānara

In the past, there was in the Himalayas a pack of monkeys that used to go to a great lake to drink water. In this lake there was an aquatic monster; whoever went there to drink water whether deer, birds, monkeys, or men were devoured by this rākṣasa. The chief of the monkeys was surprised to find the number of monkeys decreased each time when the troop returned from the lake after drinking water. At last, he found out the cause and warned his companions and advised them to drink water by means of reeds held from good distance from the bank. Buddha was the chief of the monkeys and Māra, the rākṣasa.

On another occasion, the monkey-chief with his troops eating various fruits of the Himalayas during summer became thirsty and came to the lake to drink water. He stepped on a stone which, however, got broken and he fell into the water, quite close to the hole of an ajagara (boa constrictor) which was ready to devour him. In order to find a point of support he directed the attention of the snake towards his companions. No sooner did the snake turn its neck than the chief of the monkeys stepped on its hood, jumped on the bank and escaped. (Cf. Vānara Jātaka, Jātaka, Vol. III.)

The Story of Puṇyavanta

In ancient times, there reigned in Kāśī a powerful King, named Añjana. Puṇyavanta was his only son. He used to praise good deeds and had four comrades who were the sons of the ministers of the king. They, too, in their turn used to speak highly of prowess, art, form (rūpa), and wisdom (prajñā). These five friends came to Kampilla from Benares to know who amongst them was specially respected. They came out of the town and reached the banks of the Ganges. They found a piece of wood drifting along the stream. Vīryavanta exhibiting his prowess took it ashore and found it to be a piece of sandal wood. He sold it to dealers in perfumes and spices for a thousand purāṇas (a measure equal to 16 paṇas).

Śilpavanta showed his skill in art. He played upon a lute. The people of Kampilla had never listened to such a captivating lute (a seven-stringed musical instrument). One of the strings of the lute was torn yet the ringing sound of the lute continued in the same strain. Gradually the other six strings were torn yet the lute continued to sound. Every body was astonished. Śilpavanta was amply rewarded with gold. Rūpavanta was walking in his garden and he was seen by the foremost harlot of the city. Being enchanted by his handsome appearance the harlot sent her maid to him. Later, she pleased Rūpavanta in various ways and gave him many gold coins.

One day, a banker's son wanted to take the harlot away for the night but she having been engaged previously, could not accept the invitation. Next morning the whore came to the banker's son. On being told that she had been enjoyed by him in a dream on the previous night, the prostitute demanded her fees. The banker's son having refused to pay anything, a dispute arose between them. No one could settle it. At length, Prajñāvanta happened to come there. He was appointed arbiter by the two. He took a thousand gold coins and a mirror. He showed the reflection of gold coins on the mirror to the prostitute and asked her to take the coins. Every body was pleased with his decision. Prajñāvanta was paid much gold and the prostitute went away with a broken heart.

Prince Puṇyavanta, too, went out to try his luck. While he was strolling about in the street near the palace, he was seen by the minister's son who became compassionate to him, invited him, and fed him to his satisfaction. After meal, while he was sleeping in the royal carriage-shed, the princess came there and taking him to be the minister's son waited for his waking up. But Puṇyavanta did not awake and the princess fell asleep. At sunset, the ministers saw her leaving the carriage-shed and finding Puṇyavanta asleep there took him to King Brahmadatta. Prince Puṇyavanta acquainted the King with his descent and told the truth. The minister's son and the princess supported Puṇyavanta. Then King Brahmadatta was very pleased with Prince Puṇyavanta and gave the princess in marriage to him. The King had no son. He installed Puṇyavanta on the throne. Puṇyavanta won a princess and the kingdom. Prajñāvanta was Sāriputra and Puṇyavanta was the Buddha.

The Story of Vijitāvī

In the past, there lived in Mithilā a famous king, named Vijitāvī. Every thing he had was at the disposal of brahmins and śramaṇas. The royal treasury was depleted by his unbounded charity. He was banished from the kingdom at the concerted action of the princes, prime-ministers, astrologers, citizens, merchants, etc. He took his abode in a leaf-hut near the Himalayas. Here, too, he used to collect fruits and vegetables and feed the ṛṣis before taking his own food. To test him, Indra appeared before him and began to speak ill of charity. He created a hell and made him understand that the miserable plight of the creatures in hell was due to their charity. The king could not believe in Indra's words. He said that he would gladly suffer in hell for the pleasure derived from charity. At this Indra became pleased with him and disclosing his indentity went away to heaven. A great famine, drought, rebellion, etc., visited Mithilā just on the exile of the king. Then the leading people of the country went to the forest, begged pardon of the king, and brought him back to Mithilā which soon regained her former peaceful state.

The story of the five hundred merchants and the rākṣasīs

In the past, five hundred merchants made a sea-voyage for trade from Jambudvīpa. They were shipwrecked, but living on vegetables they succeeded in saving their lives and came to an island inhabited by female demons. They were treated to various edibles and drinks and were kept there by the female demons as their husbands. The merchants lived there comfortably in the company of these female demons. They were allowed to go everywhere except to the south. One day, a merchant stealthily went to the south and saw a city surrounded by a wall made of copper. The city had no outlet. The merchant climbed a tree standing close to the wall and saw many people crying. On enquiry, he learnt from them that those females were demons who had received them with great respect but had confined them after getting new merchants; that for want of food they were on the point of death. The merchant thought of the fate of his company and himself when the female demons would get new band of merchants. He then enquired of the confined merchants as to the means of getting rid of these female demons. The imprisoned merchants advised the merchant to attend to the call of aśvarāja (king of horses), named Keśī, when he would come to this island on the full moon day in the month of Kārtika and would enquire thrice from the banks as to who would like to go to Jambudvīpa. They further told him that that aśvarāja would take them to Jambudvīpa. The merchant came back and told these facts to his companions. Then, on the full moon day in the month of Kārtika, the merchants came to the banks of the sea. They found the horse, named Keśī, and entreated him to take them to Jambudvīpa. During their departure the female demons and their children entreated them to stay there but in vain. With the help of Keśī, the merchants came to Jambudvīpa. (Cf. Valāhassa Jātaka, Jātaka, Vol. II.)

Story of the Raven

In the past, there lived in Benares a King, named Brahmadatta. At this time a king of the crows, named Supātra, lived there. His wife, named Supārśvā, who was pregnant had a longing for taking royal meal. She expressed her desire to the king of the crows. The king ordered his minister to have the royal meal brought for his queen. None out of eighty thousands of crows could bring the royal meal. Then the minister-crow himself executed the royal orders. Daily he used to bring a share of the royal meal from the royal kitchen. The royal cooks informed the king of the rudeness of the crow. The king ordered the covering of the kitchen with a net. The crow could not get the royal meal, so he began to pounce upon it. The king ordered that the meals should be brought covered. The crow lost all convenience, but he used to pounce upon the meal from the hands of the maid-servants when they used to carry it for the queens. By royal command the meals for the queens were also carried under cover. The king was very much annoyed with the crow and he declared a reward to be paid to one who would be able to catch the crow alive. The crow, too, being unable to get meals struck the nose of a maid-servant with his beak while she was carrying meals for the queens. At this time the maid-servant caught hold of the crow. The king asked the crow why he was creating so much annoyance. Then the minister-crow informed the king of the longing of Supārśvā in her family-way. The king was pleased with the bold answer of the crow and making arrangements for his daily taking away meal, the king left him. The crow used to eat a portion of the meal given by the royal cook and took the remainder for the queen. The crow king was Buddha, Supārśvā was Yaśodharā, Brahmadatta was Śuddhodana, and the minister-crow was Kālodāyī. (Kāka Jātaka in Pāli is different from this story.)

The Story of a female elephant

In the past, there was a mountain, called Caṇḍagiri, by the side of the Himalayas. Close by there was a great forest where a pair of elephants dwelt. Of this pair, the female elephant had a son who was greatly devoted to his blind mother and did not partake of food without giving anything to his mother. In course of time, hunters informed the king of Benares of the young elephant. The king of Benares came to the forest with his retinue and caught the animal. Gradually the animal became lean for not taking the food. The king enquired of the animal as to the cause of his hunger-strike. The young elephant told the king that his blind mother being deprived of his company was passing her days in grief. The king was greatly pleased with the animal for his devotion to his mother and released him. The young elephant came to the forest and shouted loudly in quest of his mother. The mother, too, understood the voice of his son and shouted at the top of her voice. Following the course of his mother's voice the young elephant came to his mother. On seeing his mother rolling in dust, the young elephant washed her with the water of the lake. His mother's blindness disappeared, and she got back her sight. Then she saw her son and became greatly delighted. She heard every thing from her young one and blessed the king of Benares.

The female elephant was Mahāprajāpatī Gautamī, king of Benares was Nanda, and the young elephant was the Buddha.

Nalinī Jātaka

In the past, there was to the north of Kāśī, by the side of the Himalayas, a hermitage called Sāhañjanī. In that hermitage there lived a sage named Kāśyapa. One day the sage committed nuisance on a slab of stone. The urine was mixed with sperm. A female deer drank it taking it to be water and licked the passage of her vulva with her tongue. The sperm of the sage got into her womb and she conceived. In course of time she gave birth to a young one in human form. The sage learnt every thing by meditation. Placing the child on a piece of deer skin the sage took him to his hermitage. The female deer followed the sage. The child was washed and cleaned by the sage. The female deer used to stroll about near the hermitage and suckled the child. The child gradually grew up, and a horn appeared on his forehead. The sage named him Ekaśṛṅga who used to wander about in the company of the female deer and other young antelopes and then returned to the hermitage. Antelopes and various birds used to join in pastime with him. When Ekaśṛṅga grew up, he used to wait upon the sage in various ways and to take his meal after feeding his mother.

The sage taught him four kinds of meditation and five supernatural faculties which he acquired in a short time. He became a brahmacārī (a celibate).

At this time, the king of Benares having had no son, performed various religious sacrifices in expectation of a son, but in vain. His only daughter, Nalinī, had by this time attained youth. The king of Benares heard of Ekaśṛṅga and intended to marry his daughter to the latter so that he might treat Ekaśṛṅga as his son or son-in-law. Then he sent his daughter with the royal priest to the Sāhañjanī hermitage. The priest took rice and sweetmeats and came by a chariot to the hermitage with princess Nalinī. There, in the hermitage, the princess began to play with her attendants. Their pastime frightened birds and antelopes who fled in various directions. While enquiring about the cause of fear of the animals Ekaśṛṅga came to Nalinī. Seeing the princess dressed in precious clothes and decked with ornaments, Ekaśṛṅga said, "Beautiful are these sons of sages, beautiful is their matted hair, beautiful are their deer skins, waistbands, and the strings of beads worn round their neck". Nalinī took Ekaśṛṅga by the hand and gave him sweets and drink. Ekaśṛṅga said that he had never partaken of such fruits and drink. The princess showed the chariot to Ekaśṛṅga and asked him to get into it which was her hermitage. Ekaśṛṅga found the horses, the carriers of the chariot, to be like his mother and did not get into the chariot. The princess embraced and kissed Ekaśṛṅga who was astonished to gaze at her person. Mutual conversation resulted in love between them. The princess tempted Ekaśṛṅga with various edibles and drink, and returned to Benares. Ekaśṛṅga came back to his hermitage. He was attached to the princess. He began to think of her and could not perform his daily duties. On being questioned, Ekaśṛṅga said every thing to the sage Kāśyapa who made him understand that his acquaintances were women, that sages should not be friendly with them, that they were obstacles to asceticism, and that their company should be given up.

By this time a large boat was beautifully decorated with flowers and fruit-trees. The boat looked like a hermitage. It sailed to Benares with the princess Nalinī, in charge of the royal priest. On reaching Benares, Nalinī alighted from the boat and entering the hermitage she began to pluck flowers and tear off leaves. The birds of the hermitage got frightened and made noise. Ekaśṛṅga came there and was glad to see the princess. Nalinī, too, was glad to see Ekaśṛṅga, embraced him, kissed him, and received him with refreshments. The princess with Ekaśṛṅga came to Benares by boat. The royal priest performed the marriage ceremony of princess Nalinī with

Ekaśṛṅga who took the princess to be his friend and began to sport with her. With the princess Ekaśṛṅga again came back to the Sāhañjani hermitage. In reply to the question put by the female deer as to where he had gone, Ekaśṛṅga said that he had accompanied his friend, Nalinī, to her hermitage and that he had accepted her hand after circumambulating fire. The female deer understood every thing and thought that her son was yet ignorant of the distinction between a friend and a wife.

Once Ekaśṛṅga wanted to enter the hermitage of female ascetics on the banks of the Ganges, near Sāhañjani hermitage, but he was prevented from doing so by the ladies of the hermitage on the ground that he was a male. On being asked by Ekaśṛṅga to explain the distinction between male and female, the ladies of the hermitage narrated feminine virtues and said that Nalinī was not his friend but a woman and that she should not be separated when already married.

Then Ekaśṛṅga in the company of the princess came to the sage Kāśyapa and told him every thing. Kāśyapa understood that there was attachment between his son and the princess, that they had been married and that they should not live separately. With his permission Ekaśṛṅga with the princess came to Benares. The King of Benares received him with great affection and anointed him crown prince. In course of time the King of Benares died. Ekaśṛṅga succeeded to the title. By his wife, Nalinī, he had 32 twin sons and by other wives he had 100 sons.

Ekaśṛṅga ruled over his kingdom righteously, and in course of time, he installed his eldest son to the throne and himself became a religious mendicant. By virtue of penance, he acquired four kinds of meditation and five supernatural faculties. After death, he was re-born in the Brahma world.

Kāśyapa was Śuddhodana,
Mṛgī was Mahāprajāpatī,
Kāśīrāja was Mahānāma Śākya,
Ekaśṛṅga was Buddha,
Nalinī was Yaśodharā (cf. Ekaśṛṅgāvadānam of the Avadānakalpalatā, and Nalinikā Jātaka, Jātaka, Vol. V).

Story of Padmāvatī

In ancient times, there lived in a great forest near the Himalayas, a hermit named Māṇḍavya. Once the sage passed urine mixed with sperm on a slab of stone. A thirsty female deer, while in her courses, drank the urine of the sage and licked the passage of her vulva with her tongue. Consequently she conceived and in due course she gave birth to a beautiful daughter. The wise sage understood every thing by meditation and brought the child to his hermitage, placing it on a piece of deer skin. The female deer followed him. Sucking her mother's breast and eating fruits given by the sage, the girl continued to grow up. When she learnt to walk, a lotus rose up from the ground under each of her foot-steps by virtue of good deeds done by her in her previous births; and she used to sport with lotuses. The sage noticed these and named her Padmāvatī.

Padmāvatī used to stroll about and play near the hermitage in the company of antelopes. She also used to follow her mother, wherever she grazed. When she grew up, she used to gather fruits, bring water, keep the hermitage clean and tidy and wait upon the sage. One day while Padmāvatī had gone to bring water, she was seen by Brahmadatta, king of Kampilla, who happened to come there in course of his hunting excursion. King Brahmadatta learnt from Padmāvatī that she was the daughter of the sage, Māṇḍavya, and conceived the desire to have her as his wife. Seeing her ignorance and knowing how she took him for some hermit, he made her taste some cakes that he was carrying away on his saddle and sent her to her father to tell him that she had liked to be the wife of the sage in whose hermitage such sweetmeats were available. Padmāvatī requested him to wait till her return with the sage's permission. The sage on hearing her words understood every thing and told Padmāvatī that she had been tempted by the fruit of Kāma (sensual desire). Padmāvatī was, however, too simple to understand the meaning of Kāma which she took to mean a tree and she wanted the fruit of this tree, she informed the ṛṣi that the donor of sweetmeats had been waiting near the tank. The saint took Padmāvati to King Brahmadatta and gave her away in marriage to the latter.

King Brahmadatta saluted the saint and taking Padmāvatī on horseback started for Kampilla. On his way home he was received by his army. Leaving the horse, he rode on elephant back and reached his country. He showed the palaces to Padmāvatī and said that these were thatched cottages and explained the noise of the city to be the howlings of wild animals. Padmāvatī believed every thing and was accompanied by the king to the pleasure garden where both the king and Padmāvatī performed a sacrifice. The king married Padmāvatī, while Padmāvatī was circumambulating fire with the king, each of her footsteps brought forth a lotus from the ground. The subjects were struck with wonder and admiration to see this.

In course of time Padmāvatī conceived. Other queens envied the respectful treatment accorded to her by the king. At the moment of her confinement they tied up her eyes with a piece of cloth. When twin sons were born they were placed in a basket (marked with royal insignia) which was consigned to the current of the Ganges. Padmāvatī's face was daubed with blood by her co-wives, and she was told that she had brought forth two flowers. The king, however, learnt on enquiry that Padmāvatī had given birth to twin sons but she had devoured them. The king saw Padmāvatī and found her face blood-stained. He took her to be a demoness and ordered her execution. The ministers came to know of the true affairs, and concealing Padmāvatī, informed the king that his orders had been executed. The harem was delighted.

A divine revelation acquainted the king with the whole affair. The king enquired of the inmates and was greatly afflicted with sorrow to hear of the true affair.

By this time, fishermen while catching fish got a basket with twin sons marked with royal insignia. The king fainted away to see the children. The ministers saw the king in this sad plight and brought Padmāvatī before the king who received her with great care and honour and expressed sorrow for the past events. Padmāvatī took the whole affair to be the fruit of her karma (deeds) and recollecting the words of the sage Māṇḍavya, she gave up "Kāmaphala" (the fruit of sensual desire) and took to ascetic life.

In the dress of a female ascetic, Padmāvatī came to her father's hermitage and learnt that the sage had died long ago, and found the cottage broken. Then Padmāvatī, in course of her round in villages and cities for alms, reached Benares, the capital of King Kṛki who tried his utmost to tempt Padmāvatī, but in vain. Ascetic Padmāvatī, however, began to stay in the palace. By this time Brahmadatta, king of Pañcāla, came to the palace of the king of Benares in the guise of a brāhmaṇa; when the king was engaged in playing at dice with his queens, Brahmadatta in the guise of a brahmin recognised Padmāvatī and asked her why she had come there. Padmāvatī replied that her arrival was due to his fault. The king of Benares heard of their conversation and became suspicious. On learning Brahmadatta's identity, he received him with great respect. Brahmadatta, king of Pañcāla, took Padmāvatī on the back of an elephant and with fourfold army came again to the city of Pañcāla. On reaching Kampilla each of Padmāvatī's steps brought forth lotus. The production of lotus under each of Padmāvatī's steps from the ground alludes to the following event. While Padmāvatī in her previous birth was bringing water, she met a Pratyeka-Buddha on the way, and offered him the lotus which was in her hand, but she took the lotus back and again presented the Pratyeka-Buddha with it once for all. For her offering lotus to the Pratyeka-Buddha, Padmāvatī acquired the merit whereby lotus used to appear under each of her steps from the ground, but she had to suffer affliction in the middle of her life for having taken the lotus back from the Pratyeka-Buddha.

Buddha = Māṇḍavya : Yaśodharā = Padmāvatī : Śuddhodana = Brahmadatta.

Story of Sūrya and Candra

In ancient times, there lived in Mithilā a Brahmin king who had two sons named Sūrya and Candra. On the death of the Brahmin King, Candra asked his brother, Sūrya, to rule over the kingdom as he was the eldest. Sūrya asked his brother to explain the duties of a king. Candra said that a king should issue orders to his subjects. Then Sūrya said that as a king he was issuing orders to his brother to govern the kingdom and that he himself would become a religious mendicant. Thus settled Sūrya, installed his brother Candra on the throne, and he himself and his family renounced worldly life. Very soon they acquired four stages of mystic meditation and five supernatural faculties. Then Sūrya decided that he would not use tooth-stick and drink water not given to him.

Once by mistake the sage Sūrya drank water from the vessel of another sage. Later, he remembered that he had done wrong and had become a thief. He came down from his seat and sat down on the ground. When his disciples came to salute him, he asked them not to do so and told them all about his stealing. His disciples endeavoured to make him understand that his act had not amounted to theft. But he could not settle his mind. He became eager for receiving punishment.

Advised by his disciples, he came to King Candra to receive punishment. He asked the king not to salute him when the latter was about to do so. On his expressing the desire of receiving punishment, the king did not consent to inflict any punishment on him. But the stubbornness of the sage constrained the king to comply with his request in consultation with his son and nephew.

The king ordered the internment of the sage in the well-docorated Aśoka forest provided with various kinds of food and sweetmeats. After six days' internment the sage Sūrya was released and he came back to his hermitage. It was Rāhula who was then Candra. It was for these six days of seclusion that he had inflicted on Bhagavat (Sūrya) that he was condemned to remain six years in his mother's breast.

Upāli

Upāli, a barber's son, was the barber of the Lord. The Śākya lads gave away their clothes to Upāli. On seeing this, Upāli became a protégé of the Buddha and took holy orders. Then five hundred Śākya lads took holy orders and by order of the Lord, they bowed down to Upāli. Their conceit and pride disappeared. King Śuddhodana too, with the members of his family, bowed down to Upāli.

The bhikkhus marked the honour received by Upāli of low caste and enquired of the Buddha about the reason thereof. The Buddha narrated the history of his previous birth.

Story of Gaṅgapāla

In ancient times, there lived in Benares two poor boys. One day taking sour gruel they went to a forest to gather fuel. At this time a Pratyeka-Buddha was entering Benares on his round for alms. On seeing him, the two boys were greatly delighted and poured their gruel on the pot of the Pratyeka-Buddha. One of them thought that he would be re-born as a king by virtue of the merit acquired by that gift. The other intended to come of a brahmin family in consequence of this gift.

As a result of their good deeds, both of them were re-born as desired. The brahmin's son, Upaka, was attached to a certain Sūdra woman. During the festival known as Kaumudī Cāturmāsī,[1] the Sūdra woman prayed to Upaka for a scented flower-garland. Upaka received from a certain person some māṣakalāi[2] which he left on the banks of the Ganges. One noon, while he was singing songs on his way to the Ganges for bringing Māṣakalāi, King Brahmadatta heard of Upaka's song from the upstairs of his palace and was pleased with him probably because of his friendship with him in a previous birth. On learning the reason of his singing songs at mid-day, King Brahmadatta wanted to give him some māṣakalāi. But Upaka did not stop. Then the king gave him half of his kingdom. Both of them began to pass their days happily.

One day, while Brahmadatta was fast asleep placing his head on the lap of Upaka, the latter first thought of acquiring kingdom by taking away the life of Brahmadatta but on a further reflection he found that that would be an act of

---

[1] It is a religious vow observed for four months commencing from the twelfth or fifteenth day of the light fortnight in the month of Āṣāḍha to the twelfth day of the light fortnight in the month of Kārtik.

[2] A sort of pulse (Phaseolus Radiatus).

ingratitude towards one who had given him half of one's kingdom. Thereafter the thought of the renunciation of worldly life crossed his mind. On Brahmadatta's waking up, Upaka told him every thing and became a religious monk.

At that time there lived in the north of Kāśī, a wandering ascetic (by caste potter) possessed of five supernatural faculties. Upaka came to him and was ordained. In course of time he became a ṛṣi by virtue of deep meditation. Brahmadatta heard of Upaka's having become a Buddhist monk, and used to say, "The condition in which I am now is the fruit of the acquisition of a very little amount of wealth. Upaka has acquired a vast amount of riches. The greatest gain is in the lot of one who receives ordination after annihilating desires." The royal inmates could not understand Brahmadatta's words.

The king had a barber named Gaṅgapāla. He was very pleased with his handicrafts and desired to reward him with a village. At the advice of the royal inmates, the barber wanted to know the meaning of the king's words instead of a village. The king narrated in detail the events connected with the life of Upaka. The royal inmates then uttered the king's words, and wanted to give valuable ornaments to Gaṅgapāla who, however, being greatly moved to hear of Upaka, came to the latter and received ordination from him. In course of time Gaṅgapāla became a great ṛṣi.

Sometime after, King Brahmadatta with his ministers came to the hermitage of Gaṅgapāla to pay him respects. Gaṅgapāla addressed the king by his name. This enraged the ministers but they touched the feet of Gaṅgapāla and sat on one side when the influence of penance was explained to them by the king.

Upaka was Buddha,
Brahmadatta was Śuddhodana,
Gaṅgapāla was Upāli.

The story of Mahāgovinda

While the Lord was on the Gṛdhrakūṭa, the Gandharva Pañcaśikha[1] came to relate to him what he had heard from the mouth of Śakra and Brahmā. The Gods, seeing new comers among them surpass the old ones by their various privileges and being informed that they were auditors of the Buddha, expressed the vow that there might be more than one Buddha at a time, in order that the benefits of his mission might have multiplied; Śakra told them that it was impossible that there might be more than one Buddha at a time. Śakra demonstrated to the devas the eight marvellous privileges (dharmas) of the Buddha, the grace of the benefits that he gave to the beings, the virtues of the law that he taught, the loneliness in which he lived dispersing his disciples and living in lonely places, his indifferences to all sensuality in the food, the great

[1] Cf. Mahāgovinda suttanta of the Dīgha Nikāya, Vol. II.

intelligence which directs his instructions, his enfranchisement of all doubt, and the perfection of his word. Śakra said that he had never found these superiorities, but in the perfectly accomplished Buddha alone. He entertained the gods by repeating to them this statement a second and then a third time.

The great Brahmā narrated the story of Mahāgovinda in order to teach the gods the "Great exposition" (mahāprajñapti) of the Buddha.

Formerly reigned the King Diśāmpati. He had, for his priest and chief adviser, a wise and intelligent brāhmaṇa named Govinda. On the death of Govinda, the king was greatly afflicted with sorrow, and was advised by his son, Prince Renu, to appoint Govinda's son, named Jyotipāla, who was more learned and skilful than his father. The king sent a messenger to invite him. Jyotipāla came to the king and accepted the royal offer of the post of his deceased father. He was then called Mahāgovinda.

On the death of Diśāmpati, six Kṣatriya royal electors (rājakartārā) assured the inheritance of the kingdom to Prince Renu with the promise of dividing the kingdom among the seven of them. The moment came and Mahāgovinda proceeded with the division of the land, assigning to each his capital. He remained in charge of all their business and instructed seven hundred brāhmaṇas and the same number of Snātakas who spread the rumour that Mahāgovinda had become familiar with Brahmā and had followed his advice. Mahāgovinda grew jealous of justifying such a favourable opinion and strenuously devoted himself during the four rainy months to deep meditation at the end of which Brahmā appeared to him. As Brahmā promised him to answer his questions, Mahāgovinda inquired of the way of obtaining Brahmaloka. Brahmā explained to him that a man could reach the immortal Brahmaloka by leaving off egotism, by concentrating his mind, by being kind, retired, without sin and deprived of sexual pleasures. Mahāgovinda was greatly moved and embraced the life of a hermit.

Then follow accounts of the rewards received by the disciples of Mahāgovinda, and of chastisements to those who brought opposition to Mahāgovinda or to his disciples. In course of time Pañcaśikha acquired insight into the Dharma, Buddha was at that time Mahāgovinda.

While the Buddha was once staying at Śrāvastī in the Jetavana Vihāra of Anāthapiṇḍika, he passed three months there with one dish of food per diem. He declared to Ānanda that he could have lived in this way during whole Kalpas; for such was the privilege of the exactly accomplished Buddhas who had attained the pāramitās (perfections).[1]

---

[1] There are ten pāramitās or perfections:—

(1) Dāna (almsgiving), (2) sila (morality), (3) nekkhamma (renunciation of the world), (4) paññā (wisdom), (5) viriya (energy), (6) khanti (forbearance), (7) sacca (truthfulness), (8) adhiṭṭhāna (resolution) (9) mettā or metti (friendliness), and (10) upekkhā (indifference).

He further said that, an infinite number of Kalpas ago, there lived the Buddha Indradhvaja in his capital, Indratapana. He then enumerated a long series of Buddhas, viz., Mahādhvaja, Dhvajottama, Dhvajarucira, Dhvajaketu, Ketudhvaja, Dhvajodhvaja, Dhvajamaparājita, Aparājita, Supratāpa, Badīpa, Supratiṣṭhita, Nāgamuni, Mahāmuni, Munipravara, Saṁvṛtaskandha, Vandhuma, Ariṣṭa, Vijitāvi, Krakucchanda, Asamsama, Prabhaṁkara, Anghaja, Mahāvala, Sujāta, Paraṁgata, Mahāprasāda, Sukhendriya, Nakṣattrarāja, Śatapuṣpa, Viraja, Brahmasvara, Śirasāhwaya who lived in his capital named Puspāvatī, Nāgakulottama, Kṣamottara, Nāgottama, Aṅgottama, Vāsava, Candrima, Hetumanta, Jinendra, Jāmbunada, Tagarasikhi, Paduma, Kauṇḍinyagotra Candana, Viraja, Hitesī, Supātra who lived in his capital Abhayapura, Varunottama, Dhṛtarāṣṭra, Śveturāṣṭra, Śikhi, Viruḍaka, Sunetra, Sujāta, Utpala, Brahmottama, Sudarśana, Arthdarśī, Mūla, Anṣaḍī, Hitaiṣī, Jāmbunada, Sāla, Abhiji, Jinávaruttama, Samaṁtabhadra, Śaśīvimala, Pauṇḍarika, Candrima, Bhāvitmā, Oghaja, Abhaya, Svayaṁprabha, Mahāvala, Āditya, Pratāpavanta, Hiteṣī, Dhvajottama, Dhvajadhvaja, Ketu, Ketuttama, Asahya, Jāmbunada, Sālarāja, Akutobhaya, Nirmita, Upaśānta, Jinendra, Sarvārthadarśī, Aśoka, Dhvajottama, Nyagrodharāja, Bipulajaśa, Jayanta, Śākyamuni who lived in his capital Sinhapuri, Sarvaḍaya, Atyuttama, Uttara, Samitāvi, Valadatta, Bhāgīratha, Aṅgīrasa, Nāgottama, Nāgavala, Puṣpa, Puṣputtara,

Meru, Ratnāgni, Puṣpakṛta, Dīpaṅkara, who lived in his capital Dīpavatī, Sarvābhibhu, Padumuttara, Atyuccagāmi, Yaśottara, Śākyamuni, Arthadarśī, Tiṣya, Puṣya, Vipaśyi, Sikhi, Viśvabhuva, Krakucchanda, Konākamuni, Kāśyapa, Śākyamuni, Maitreya in his capital Ketumati.

Thereafter, Ānanda asked the Exalted one how he had acquired the splendour with which he used to illuminate the world. The Lord said that it was through the respects he had paid to the ancient Buddhas from Dīpaṅkara to Kāśyapa. On being questioned by Ānanda as to when and for how long these Buddhas had lived, the Lord explained to him by turn that every one of these Buddhas had gone up to a number of Kalpas—the time that each one had spent on earth. He further explained the etymology of the names of the former Buddhas as well as the future Buddha, Maitreya, the class, Kṣatriya or Brāhmaṇa to which each one of the Buddhas belonged, according to circumstances.

The Story of Rāhula

The Buddha, staying in the atmosphere, showed various miracles. Chiefs of Asuras, Rāhu, Vemacitrī Mucilinda together with their companions were initiated into the Dharma. King Śuddhodana saw these miracles and with folded hands he said to the Lord, "I have gained much as I have got you as my son. Your renunciation of kingdoms and relations has been successful. Your meditation for six years has been crowned with success, and my birth has met with success inasmuch as I was blessed with a child like you. Take your food in the palace for the days you will be here in Kapilavastu." The town was well decorated. Various edibles were arranged. The Buddha entered the town with Sāriputra in his right, Maudgalyāyana on his left, and with Ānanda behind him. Horses neighed while entering into the city. The peacocks danced, and cuckoes cooed. Various instruments were played. The blind regained eyesight. The deaf got back the sense of hearing. The insane regained their lost memory. All sorts of evil disappeared. The irreverent began to respect their superiors. The earth quaked. The Buddha entered the palace. The Śākyas declared that capital punishment would be inflicted on those who would speak out the Buddha's identity to Rāhula. The Lord used to take his meal in the palace. Mahāprajāpatī Gotamī invited him with the bhikkhus. Various edibles were brought. The house was well-decorated. The Buddha and the bhikkhus took their seats. Mahāprajāpatī Gotamī herself served the dinner. The Buddha gave religious instructions to Mahāprajāpatī Gotamī and other inmates. Rāhula took his seat where the shadow of the Buddha fell.

He gazed steadfastly at the Buddha. He asked his mother where his father was.

Yaśodharā said, "Your father has gone to the Deccan" (Dakṣiṇāpatha).

Rāhula said, "Why has he gone there?"

Yaśodharā said, "To trade".

Rāhula said, "Why does not my father send some good articles?"

Yaśodharā said, "It is against the custom of the Kṣatriyas. He will bring articles when he will come".

Rāhula said, "Is this Sramaṇa a relation of ours? I am getting interested in him. He appears to be lkie my father."

Yaśodharā said, "No, he is not your father".

Rāhula said, "Tell me please truly what he is to me".

Yaśodharā was moved. She neglected the declaration of capital punishment and said, "Yes, this Śramaṇa is your father". Rāhula caught hold of the outskirts of the Buddha's robe and said that he would enter the holy orders if the Śramaṇa was his father and that he would follow his father's footsteps. The inmates cried. King Śuddhodana heard of this cry and learnt every thing on enquiry. His eyes were full of tears. He bowed down to the Buddha and prayed for Rāhula. His prayer was not granted. Buddha said that Rāhula was, by virtue of the merits acquired by him in his previous births, destined to attain Nirvāṇa. In seven days, the ceremonies of Jātakarna (the first of the ten purification ceremonies performed shortly after birth), of first tonsure and Kuntalavardhana (ceremony for the growth of long hair) were performed. Yaśodharā spoke to him about the sufferings of the hermit-life, and also about the enjoyment of royal happiness. She tried her utmost to restrain Rāhula from entering holy orders. But all was in vain. Yasódharā marked his determination and gave him advice.

By order of king Śuddhodana the city of Kapilavastu was adorned. Prince Rāhula entered the holy order and accepted discipleship of his father. The Lord received him with tenderness and some words of exhortation. He charged Sāriputra to ordain Rāhula who repeated the triśaraṇa and the daśaśila. The barber cut Rāhula's hair, whilst the Lord exhorted him to perfection. Yaśodharā sadly touched the hair that had been cut off from her son, while she lamented. Maudgalyāyana and Sāriputra conferred the ordination on the young prince, Rāhula; under the direction of Sāriputra, he began his monastical career. On the last day Yaśodharā invited the Buddha.

She prepared a brilliant reception and tried to seduce him and to change his dispositions by the jewels with which she adorned herself and the daintiness that she offered to him; but all was of no avail. The Lord went away after having informed the King and the women.

The Lord attained Perfect Enlightenment and stayed underneath the Bodhi-tree for a week. Gods showered flowers from heaven. All creatures worshipped the Buddha. Gazing steadfastly at the Bodhi-tree for a week he passed the second week there with a cheerful heart. In the third week, Tandri and Arati, daughters of Māra, seeing their father lamenting over his defeat, forced themselves in spite of the disappointing advice of their father to triumph over the Buddha, firstly by sensuality, by surrounding them with seducing apparitions to which the Buddha remained indifferent; then by asking him questions to which he replied in such a way as to confound them. They went away defeated and Māra proclaimed their defeat.

Story of Dharmalabdha

Kāla, king of the snakes, came to the Buddha and told him that previous Buddhas used to go to his abode. He invited the Buddha who came to Kāla's house and spent the fourth week. At the request of Mucilinda, king of the snakes, the Buddha spent the fifth week at his house. With his hood, Mucilinda protected the Buddha from the untimely shower during the whole week. The sixth week the Buddha spent under the Nyagrodha tree. The seventh week he spent in the Khīrikāvana at the Vahudeva Caitya. Thus the Buddha spent seven weeks without any food.

Story of Trapusa and Bhallika

At this time, Trapusa and Bhallika, two merchants, while coming from Utkal (Orissa) came to grief near Khīrikāvana. They were greatly frightened but gods favoured them with assurance of security and asked them to offer the Buddha his first food, the delicious madhutarpana, after his forty-nine days' fast. The Buddha was thinking of taking them. Just at this time four Mahālokapālas brought four plates. As soon as the four plates were taken by the Buddha, they merged into one. The Buddha took honeyed butter on the plate and recited the "Svastika maṅgala", the stanzas of blessing which protect in all regions. The two merchants received the Triśaraṇa, and begged of the Buddha some articles for worship. The Buddha gave them as relics, some hair from his head and some clippings of nails from his fingers. On these relics, the two merchants built in Keśasthali the Keśastūpa (hair stūpa), at Bālukṣa the Nakhastūpa (nail stūpa), at Silukṣa, a monument, the stones of which came by themselves to be put in place, through the miraculous power of the Lord Buddha. Śakra came in his turn to offer the Buddha a haritakī of which, he planted the stalk, which, at once, transformed itself wonderfully into a tree covered with flowers and fruits. While the Buddha was engaged in deep meditation for six years at the Senāpatigāma in Uruvilvā, a public woman, named Gavā, kept a coarse cloth on the bough of a tree for Buddha's wear after meditation. By virtue of this noble deed Gavā was re-born in heaven as a nymph. At her prayer, the Buddha took that coarse cloth, rejecting the cloth given by Gods. Water was required to wash the cloth. The King of Gods dug with his hands a river which still bears the name of Pāṇikhāta. A slab of stone was required. Four lokapālas brought four pieces of stone. On one slab he washed his cloth, on the second he spread the cloth to dry, the third he threw away in the names of Trapusa and Bhallika, inhabitants of Śilukṣa-nagara, who established that piece of stone in a Caitya. Still there exists in the kingdom of Gāndhāra, a town named Śila. On the fourth the Buddha took his seat and stitched the cloth. Over these four slabs of stone four Caityas were built. The Buddha, after washing and stitching that cloth, bathed in the Pāṇikhāta river and got up from the river by holding the arm of the God Kakubha, the presiding deity of the tree named Kakubha, which stood on the banks of the river. The Buddha placed one of his hands on the tree which still bears the impression of the five fingers of the Buddha's palm. Then the Buddha took his seat underneath the Nyagrodha tree of the goat-herd. He made up his mind to keep his Doctrine to himself as it was too deep to be understood and accepted by the world.

Knowing the Buddha's dispositions, Brahmā with Śakra and other Gods came to request him to promulgate his doctrine, but they went away disappointed.

At that time, false doctrines reigned at Magadha; Brahmā took the opportunity of requesting Buddha to enlighten men. The Buddha reflected that out of the three species of beings, who were quite in the wrong, or quite in the right, or who were not exclusively enfeoffed either to the one or to the other, the third at least would profit by his instructions. Remembering his past resolutions and yielding to the petition of the gods, Buddha promised to turn the Wheel of Law. From heaven to heaven the news spread up to the Brahmaloka. Then he looked for him who was able to follow his instruction. He thought of preaching his dharma to Udraka Rāmaputra but afterwards he learnt that Udraka had passed away seven days ago. Then he thought of Ārāḍa Kālāma and came to know that he too had died three days ago. Then he found that those who had followed him during his austerities were the five Bhadravargiyas who were at that time staying at Ṛṣipatana Mṛgadāva at Benares. He intended to preach dharma to these persons. From Bodhi he proceeded towards Benares. Gods adorned with magnificent splendour the road that separated the Bodhi from Benares. From Uruvilvā, the Buddha came to Gayā, from Gayā to Apara Gayā where he was invited by Sudarśana, king of snakes. The Buddha took his meal there and came to Vaśālā where he preached his doctrine to a Brāhmaṇa, named Nadi. A householder of Vaśālā gave him cloth. From Vaśālā he went to a city named Cundadvīla, where he announced to the Ājīvaka named Upaka, that, without a master, he had become an Arhat, Jina, and Buddha, and that he would promulgate the law. Buddha was invited by Cunda and passed one night in his house. From Cundadvīla he came to Lohitavastuka where he passed one night as a guest of Kamaṇḍaluka, king of snakes. From Lohitavastuka he came to Gandhapura when he was invited by the Yakṣa named Kandha. After halting there for one night he came to Sārathipura and from Sārathipura he came to the banks of the Ganges. The boatman did not agree to take him free. So Buddha crossed the Ganges like a duck and reaching Benares he waited at Saṅkhamedhī till the hour for begging in the town had come. On coming back from his round, he came to Ṛṣipatana and was cordially received by the five Bhadravargiyas named Ājñātakauṇḍinya, Aśvaka, Bhadraka, Vāṣpa, and Mahānāma who in spite of their concerted project, could not help standing up at his approach and were ordained monks by the Buddha. Buddha recognised the place where the former Buddhas had made the Wheel of the Law turn. He enumerated to the five monks the dimensions of the nimbuses of a certain number of Buddhas. He instructed the five monks about the middle path and āryasatya (perfect truth). The sight of the Law was revealed to Kauṇḍinya and to eighteen koṭis of devas. At Benares, Buddha taught the five monks that the five Skandhas (elements of being), *viz.*, Rūpa (form), Vedanā (sensation), Saṁjñā (perception), Saṅkhāras (pre-existent dispositions), and Vijñāna (consciousness) were without any substance. They are the source of torment. They are impermanent; in recognising their impermanence, the torment of which they are the source, is suppressed. Ājñātakauṇḍinya received "the privilege of strength", the four others deprived themselves forever of the āśravas, and koṭis of devas received the Enlightenment of the Law.

The Buddha, while at Ṛṣipatana, instructed the three bhikṣus (who had gone to Benares to beg) that one must consider one's self to be able to discover the source of suffering; the sufferings were discovered by recognising the impermanence of suffering. The three bhikṣus received "the privilege of strength" and eighty koṭis of devas, the pure sight of the Law.

It was on the twelfth day of the second fortnight of Āṣāḍa, the shadow having one and a half the height of the objects, under the nakṣatra, Anurādha, at the hour called Vijaya, that the Buddha turned the Wheel of the Law. The five Bhadravargiyas were converted into the Buddhist faith.

Story of Pūrṇa Maitrāyaṇiputra

Pūrṇa was the son of a rich brahmin at Droṇavastuka in Kośala. His mother was named Maitrāyaniputra. Having heard of Siddhārtha and his doctrine, Pūrṇa devoted himself to the religious life. He had twenty-nine disciples with whom he came to Ṛṣipatana. There they paid homage to the Buddha who ordained all of them and conferred on them the privilege of strength.

In the village named Markaṭa in Avanti, there

lived a rich brahmin belonging to the Kātyāyana gotra. The brahmin was the priest of the King Ujjhebhaka Toneharaka. He had two sons named Uttara and Nālaka. Uttara used to study the Vedas with his uncle Asita. Nālaka was very intelligent. He learnt the Vedas by listening to his brother's reading the Vedas. He came to Asita. Wonderfully gifted as he was, he devoted himself to the religious life under the direction of his uncle. By the permission of Asita he came to Benares where at that time six preachers, *viz.*, Pūraṇa Kāśyapa, Gosālikaputra Maṣkali, Ajita Kesakambalī, Kātyāyana Kakuda, Vairaṭikaputra Sañjayī, and Jñātriputra Nirgrantha, preached the dharma. Nālaka went to all of these preachers but none of them could satisfy him.

Story of Nālaka

At that time there were four rich men, Saṅkha at Benares, Paduma at Mithilā, Piṅgala at Kaliṅga, and Elāpatra at Takṣaśilā. Every month, they used to celebrate in Benares, a feast of the Saṅkha, one of the four great treasures, to which were invited rich nāgarājās. Elāpatra, the naga king, put to the Buddha some questions, answers to which satisfied Nālaka so much that he presented himself before Buddha and asked him to give him ordination. Once ordained Nālaka put to the Buddha some questions regarding the essential laws of religious life. These questions were answered by the Buddha. They became celebrated as Nālaka questions.

Story of Sabhika

There lived in Mathurā a rich banker who had an unlucky daughter whom he made over to a paribrājaka. The ascetic brought her up at the banker's expense and gave her religious instruction; she distinguished herself by her knowledge and cleverness in the discussions. She discussed Śāstras with the ascetics. None could defeat her. At this time a brahmin learned in all Śāstras came to Mathurā from the Deccan for discussion. It was arranged that the discussion would be held between the brahman and the girl. But before the discussion commenced, the brahmin came to see the girl and at first sight both of them felt for each other a mutual passion, and decided to pledge that one who would be defeated in discussion would submit to the winner and that the girl-ascetic would willingly be defeated, so that they could easily be united without being defamed by the public. Then the discussion continued for seven days before kings, princes, and learned men. At last the girl-ascetic willingly admitted her defeat. People declared the victory of the brahmin. The girl-ascetic in accordance with the terms of the previous arrangement with the brahmin yielded to the latter and left the place of discussion. In due course the girl ascetic conceived. Both of them started for the Deccan. In the tenth month of her pregnancy they reached Śvetavalākā where they spent the night. There the girl-ascetic brought forth a son who was named Sabhika on account of his being born in the meeting. Sabhika read all the Śāstras in his youth. When he came to the age of understanding, he looked for the Buddha every where and finally arrived at Ṛṣipatana Mṛgadāva. There Sabhika put to the Buddha some questions, answers to which pleased him, and he embraced Buddha's faith and took holy orders.

Story of Yaśoda

In Benares on the banks of the river Varaṇā, there was a huge Nyagrodha tree which granted any thing that was desired. A childlesss banker of Benares was not blessed with a child even after performing many sacrifices. Along with his wife he came to the Nyagrodha tree and prayed for a son making a vow that he would build a temple for the tree and worship it with grandeur if he were blessed with a child, otherwise he would extirpate it. The god of the tree got frightened, came to Śakra and told him of his imminent danger. Śakra ordered a god of the Trayastriṁśa heaven who was approaching the end of his divine existence, to be born as a son of the banker. This god was given the hope that he would be able to receive ordination from the Buddha. He was born of the banker and was named Yaśoda.

He passed his youthful days in great happiness, in palaces which were built for his residence during the autumn, the summer, and the rainy seasons. Thousands of wives were kept in different harems.

One day, when a householder came to their

house from the east on business, the banker was at that time in the palace on a special business. In course of his conversation with the householder, Yaśoda learnt much about the Buddha. One midnight, while the inmates were all asleep, Yaśoda left home and took refuge in the Buddha. He was given various instructions by the Buddha. He acquired knowledge and various miraculous powers.

At daybreak, Yaśoda's parents could not find their son at home. Leaving home in the company of many men in search of their son, they reached the banks of the river. There they found their son's sandals and began to cry. At length, they came to the Buddha and asked him about their son. Yaśoda was present there but no body could see him. By order of the Buddha, Yaśoda demonstrated his supernatural powers by performing all sorts of miracles, such as staying in the air, etc. The Śramaṇa Ulukapakṣikabhaginī and other heretics were astonished at the sight of these miracles. The Buddha recited two stanzas to certify that it was the internal virtue and not the external practices such as having a shaved head, or matted pair, or besmearing one's body with unguents, etc., that made a man, a true monk.

He gave various instructions to Yaśoda's parents and their companions. He discoursed on almsgiving, moral precepts, heaven, virtue, and results of virtuous deeds. He explained to them four

Vajjibhumi (Vaiśālī) as they must be sent to different countries and as they should live in isolation.

Story of three Kāśyapa brothers

The Blessed One wishing to go to Jaṭila Uruvilvā Kāśyapa created by his magical power a thousand Jaṭilas and himself in the guise of a Jaṭila took them to Uruvilvā Kāśyapa's hermitage. Kāśyapa who had five hundred Jaṭila disciples felt diffident at the sight of a thousand Jaṭilas. He was afraid lest the people should pay more respects to the chief of the thousand Jaṭilas than to him. Buddha understood the state of his mind and caused his own clothes and thousand disciples to disappear. Kāśyapa was astonished to mark the disappearance of the thousand Jaṭilas and to see the Buddha in his own countenance. He thought that his own miraculous power was greater than Gautama's. Kāśyapa thought that the people would bow down to, and worship Śramaṇa Gautama.

The Buddha understood Kāśyapa's thought and through air came to the Nyagrodha tree of Ajapāla on the banks of the river Nairañjanā, at Senāpatigrāma in Uruvilvā. When the Buddha left the hermitage, people went away. Kāśyapa wished that Śramaṇa Gautama would again come to his hermitage and take his meal there. The Buddha understood Kāśyapa's desire and returned to his hermitage. Uruvilvā

Kāśyapa thought that Śramaṇa Gautama could read the thoughts of others and that he himself possessed greater miraculous powers. With his own hand, he offered food to the Buddha. Kāśyapa and the members of his family stayed in the air and tried to perform a burnt-offering but fire did not burn. They thought, "under whose influence the fire did not burn. It must be due to the influence of Śramaṇa Gautama." Then fire burnt. They then acknowledged Śramaṇa Gautama to be the possessor of great miraculous power but they thought themselves to be superior to him. They gave offering to the fire but the offering did not fall into the fire. They thought that this was perhaps due to Gautama's influence. Then, offerings fell into the fire. At the end of the burnt-offering, Kāśyapa and the members of his family could not come down from the sky. No sooner did they think that it was due to the Buddha's influence than they were able to come down. They thought that Śramaṇa Gautama was possessed of great miraculous power, but they themselves were superior to him. When they were about to bring water they could not see the water-pot. They thought of the Buddha and found the water-pot. They went to the Nairañjanā river but they could not fill the water-pot. They remembered the Buddha's influence and the water-pot was full of water. They desired to take their meal but they could not do so. As soon as they thought of the influence of the Buddha they were able to take their food. After taking their meal, they wanted to fell wood but they could not hurl the raised axe. No sooner did they think that it was due to the influence of the Buddha than they were able to hurl the axe and fell wood. Though they acknowledged Gautama to be the possessor of great miraculous power, yet they could not but persevere in their presumption that their miraculous powers were greater than Gautama's. Then the Buddha showed five hundred miracles to the three Kāśyapa brothers. The last miracle was that the Buddha desired to lie down in the room where fire burnt. In that room there lived a wicked snake, so Kāśyapa did not approve. But as soon as the Lord left his seat and entered the fire-room, the wicked snake came to his vessel. They were struck with wonder to see the fire burn and the wicked snake in the vessel. They desired to save Gautama by extinguishing fire by water. But Gautama controlled the snake and making it free from poison held it in his vessel. Uruvilvā Kāśyapa with the disciples was astonished at this spectacle. Then Uruvilvā Kāśyapa with his five hundred disciples, Nadi Kāśyapa with his three hundred disciples, and Gayā Kāśyapa with his two hundred disciples were charmed to see the miraculous power of the Buddha and became his disciples. Their miraculous powers disappeared; they put on the robes of bhikkhus and took holy orders. Upasena, a nephew of the Kāśyapas, lived in a hermitage with three hundred disciples on the banks of the river Nairañjanā. He acquired four stages of mystic meditation, five supernatural faculties, and great miraculous power. One day, on seeing all the garments of his maternal uncles and their hermit's accessories drifting along the stream, he with his pupils ran to the hermitage of his maternal uncles. He learnt every thing about the Buddha from his maternal uncles; and with his pupils he became a disciple of the Buddha and took ordination.

In order to explain the story of the three Kāśyapas, the Blessed One related to the monks how they were formerly three brothers reigning together at Sinhapura in Kaliṅga. Their kingdoms produced many precious gems. Taking these gems they came to King Mahendra's kingdom, Hastināpura, where Buddha Puṣpa with his disciples used to dwell begging for alms. They offered these gems to King Mahendra who gladly accepted the offer and asked them what he could do for them. They expressed their desire that Buddha Puṣpa would very kindly spend the rainy season in their city. Their desire was fulfilled. Buddha Puṣpa with his disciples came to their kingdom, but during the rainy season he attained nirvāṇa there. The three Kāśyapa brothers, however, honoured his remains, and raised a stūpa thereon.

On leaving the hermitage of Uruvilvā Kāśyapa,

the Blessed One followed by his disciples, arrived at the hermitage of Dharmāraṇya, where dwelt many old and accomplished Jaṭilas. He preached to them the "Sahasravarga" of the Dharmapada and gave them the privilege of strength. They attained nirvāṇa. The Blessed One honoured their remains and built stūpas for them. He then came to the Nyagrodha of the goat-herd.

While the Buddha was staying at the foot of the Nyagrodha tree of Ajapāla, on the banks of the Nairañjanā river, the chief brahmin priest of king Bimbisāra used to repeat to him in detail the thirty-two signs of a great man every morning. The king listening to his repetitions felt like seeing a Buddha and learning his instructions.

One morning, in the company of his harem and officers, King Bimbisāra came to a neighbouring part of the town from where he could see Rājagṛha and its neighbours. The king felt a disgust for the objects of desire and thought thus, "where are the ancestors who built those beautiful palaces and pleasant ponds, etc.? Every thing is here except the ancestors who built them. Death is certain for mankind and life to the living is full of misery". One of the officers, seeing the king's melancholy, tried to cheer him up, by praising the beauty of Rājagṛha, but this helped to make him worse. The royal priest, being more inspired, spoke to the king about the Buddha. The king was highly pleased with him, praised, and rewarded him.

The Buddha with many bhikkhus came to Rājagṛha in Magadha and stayed in the garden at Yaṣṭivana on the Antagiri. King Bimbisāra heard of the Buddha's advent from his priest. The king ordered his men to decorate Rājagṛha and to make his chariots ready. The king, the prince, the ministers, the councillors, the priests, and other persons arrived at Yaṣṭivana with great splendour. They saluted the Buddha and took their seats. The people of Rājagṛha were astonished to see Uruvilvā Kāśyapa as Buddha's disciple. The Buddha understood their thoughts and had a talk with Kāśyapa. During his conversation with the Buddha, Kāśyapa recognised the inanity of his ancient customs and proclaimed that the Buddha was his master. Kāśyapa bowed down to him and paid him due respects. The people of Magadha took Kāśyapa to be a disciple of the Buddha.

The Buddha instructed the people of Rājagṛha on the source and the destruction of the Skandhas (elements). He explained to them the impermanence of rūpa, vedanā, saṁjñā, saṁskāras, and vijñāna. He asked them to leave the last path and to follow the middle path. "Saṃskāra or Saṅkhāra arises from ignorance; from Saṅkhāra springs up knowledge; thus name and form, six internal senses, perception, suffering, desire, attachment, existence, re-birth, old age, death, etc., are produced. Every thing born of ignorance is perishable." He recited to them the pratityasamutpāda (dependent origination) of the ten nidānas. At the end of the sermon a general conversation took place.

King Bimbisāra acquired knowledge on hearing Buddha's discourse. The king and his company were greatly pleased with the Buddha and praised him.

Story of King Arindama

In ancient times, there reigned in the city of Mithilā in Videha, a king named Arindama who was very prosperous and charitable. Śroṇaka, the son of the royal priest, was the king's playmate. He was learned and well versed in the three Vedas. He realised sorrow in Kāma (desire), and became a religious mendicant. He went to the Himalayas and practising penance acquired four meditations and five abhijñā (knowledge). He wished to have the king ordained. He came to the mango-grove of Mahādeva through air and took his seat underneath a mango-tree. There the royal priest observed his presence and after greeting him came to Mithilā. Just at this time the king feeling a disgust for the objects of his desire promised a reward to the one who after enquiry would acquaint him with the whereabouts of Śroṇaka. Informed by the royal priest, the king came there riding on an elephant and seeing Śroṇaka said to him, "Why do you sit underneath the tree like a poor man?" Śroṇaka said, "I am not poor in virtue. One who does not practise virtue is really poor". The king said to him "Why do you lie in forest? Why do you stay alone in the forest? Don't you feel physical discomfort? Please come with me to the city where I will protect you". Śroṇaka said, "I wander alone, what shall I do with a kingdom? This is my first happiness. I wander everywhere, nobody can oppose me. This is my second happiness. I stroll about with a pot and a mendicant's dress. This is my third happiness. If the whole of Mithilā is burnt, nothing of mine will be burnt. This is my fourth happiness." Though the wandering ascetics belonged to different families and countries, yet they loved one another. The king was greatly delighted at Śroṇaka's words and said to him, "Let the happiness of those of whom you have spoken, be eternal. We are tempted by passion. What shall we do?" Śroṇaka then narrated a story which runs thus—"In ancient times, an old elephant died on a mountain. The Ganges carried the corpse away. A raven was delighted to see the corpse. It settled on the floating corpse and began to eat its flesh and to drink the water of the Ganges alternately. It had not to labour any more to earn its bread. It therefore allowed itself, being careless of the consequence, to be carried away along with the corpse, by the current of the Ganges to the middle of the ocean where aquatic animals devoured the corpse together with the raven on it". Śroṇaka further said that those who would not observe the law would be tortured in one or other of the eight hells, *viz.*, Saṁjīva, Kālasutra, Saṃghāta, Raurava,

Mahāraurava, Avīci, Tapaṇa, and Pratāpaṇa. The king at once said that he would not imitate the foolishness of the raven, and that he would take holy orders on that very day as there was no knowing when death would snatch him away. He then sent for his son Dīrghāyu, and transferred all royal powers to him. Dīrghāyu desired to follow the example of his father but he was brought away by the royal officers. A woman of the harem wishing to retain the king tried her level best to seduce him. But the king resisted the seductions, took holy orders, and became a disciple of Śroṇaka.

INDEX